It's
NEVER
Too Late
to
FINISH
WELL

(or too early to start)

A MAN'S GUIDE TO FINISHING WELL

by Paul Goodman

Order this book online at www.trafford.com/07-1002
or email orders@trafford.com

Most Trafford titles are also available at major online book retailers.

Note for Librarians: A cataloguing record for this book is available from Library and Archives Canada at www.collectionscanada.ca/amicus/index-e.html

ISBN: 978-1-4251-7486-6

We at Trafford believe that it is the responsibility of us all, as both individuals and corporations, to make choices that are environmentally and socially sound. You, in turn, are supporting this responsible conduct each time you purchase a Trafford book, or make use of our publishing services. To find out how you are helping, please visit www.trafford.com/responsiblepublishing.html

Our mission is to efficiently provide the world's finest, most comprehensive book publishing service, enabling every author to experience success. To find out how to publish your book, your way, and have it available worldwide, visit us online at www.trafford.com/10510

 www.trafford.com

North America & international
toll-free: 1 888 232 4444 (USA & Canada)
phone: 250 383 6864 ♦ fax: 250 383 6804 ♦ email: info@trafford.com

The United Kingdom & Europe
phone: +44 (0)1865 722 113 ♦ local rate: 0845 230 9601
facsimile: +44 (0)1865 722 868 ♦ email: info.uk@trafford.com

10 9 8 7

Table of Contents

PART I

The Issues of Finishing Well

CHAPTER 1

Facing The End

Sooner or later it happens to everyone. You recognize that life has boundaries. There is a beginning and an end. Your life is played out between two points in time–birth and death. When you're young you joke about it. "The only things in life that are certain are death and taxes." It's a reality, but death seems so far off that only intellectual assent is made. There is so much to do. So much to experience. Mountains to climb.

Achievements to experience. A wife to marry. Children to raise. The future is bright and appealing. The distant horizon that holds the end of your life is too far away to worry about.

Although each individual is different in many ways, the decades of life for most men can be viewed as containing fairly predictable patterns.

Twenty-Somethings

You dig into life. When you're in your twenties the world looks like one big cookie ready to be eaten. You want to eat the whole thing and savor each bite along the way. Time isn't an issue except you want to attack life with gusto and not wait around. The road ahead looks long and clear.

Some people work hard just to enjoy whatever life brings their way—life is a party. Others don't enjoy it as much because they are consumed by worry about success and the future. However, others begin to plan what that future will bring. They look at their desires, set goals and head down their chosen path. Those who don't consciously set goals default to life's paths by the decisions they make on the short run, such as education and employment opportunities.

Those goals cover a broad landscape. Family. Career. Financial. Spiritual. Lifestyle. Some might want to climb to the top of their profession. Others dream of outer space–literally. For many it doesn't involve career because work is mainly a means to an end–making money to support a family or lifestyle. Their real goals fall into avocation areas like sports, hobbies, or other activities.

For example, you might determine that before life is over

you are going to climb all the "14ers" in Colorado. (Those are mountains over 14,000 feet tall.) Literally and figuratively there are many mountains you want to climb before your life is over.

As life goes along your experiences begin to shape your views. If you're successful, you might set your goals even higher. If you're not, you might set them lower or change them altogether.

Thirty-Somethings

When you land in the thirties you recognize there are stages or seasons to life. Most men in their thirties find themselves smack in the middle of trying to balance the demands of a rising career and a young family. They most likely enjoy the many activities and relationships with family, friends, and co-workers. However, they also might be looking forward to a time when the demands are not so broad or immediate. An empty nest begins to have some appeal.

Forty-Somethings

Somewhere in the forties the typical man begins to go through some form of midlife crisis. Because the physical issues appear minimal, it is often called a transition rather than a crisis. Although many women face significant physical issues at midlife, this time of life for men occurs more on the emotional level. (Although male menopause has been physiologically documented, it doesn't carry the immediate physical symptoms that women face.)

This midlife crisis goes hand-in-hand with the realization

that physically you are changing. All through the twenties and thirties you know you are getting older, but not much appears to change. Physically you seem to be staying pretty level. Physical fitness buffs know they aren't quite as strong or quick as they were a few years earlier, but their workouts are still vigorous and some extra time and intensity make up for what the body naturally had earlier. Those who are not into strenuous workouts may not as clearly notice the many physical changes that are taking place. Gray hair has not yet appeared for most. However, they may experience that they don't adjust to high altitudes quite as quickly when they go skiing. Or a Saturday project leaves them with sore muscles the next day. No big deal, but enough to let you know things are changing and starting to demand your attention.

What is happening on the physical side is very subtle and unnoticed by most. Starting around the age of thirty the body begins to produce lower levels of hormones. It's a slow but steady process. Most people don't realize that by the time they hit their fifties they will be producing some hormones at half the level they did at thirty.

In your late forties and early fifties it's no longer possible to ignore what is taking place. Probably the most universal sign of aging to assert itself is vision. The need for bifocals or reading glasses is an "in your face" daily reminder that things are not what they used to be.

At the same time all these physical changes are taking place there are external issues that also demand to be heard. If you have been climbing the ladder at work, you may realize that you are never going to get where you thought you were headed. What does that mean for your life? How does it affect your future?

And, even for the lucky few who make it to the top, they face the same issue only from a different perspective. They've reached their goals. They may have sold their company. The money is in the bank and now they find themselves asking, "Is this all there is?"

The majority who are not climbing the corporate ladder also experience similar challenges. The realization that your income will never be what you had hoped or dreamed becomes a slow reality. The expense of raising children, paying a mortgage, buying and maintaining automobiles seems to keep you in a perpetual state of trying to make ends meet. While you once thought that you could quit any job you didn't like and move on to another, you are beginning to realize that new jobs are not always available when you want them. You discover that many people take a pay cut when they switch jobs rather than find an increase automatically waiting for them. In addition, even though it is illegal to discriminate on the basis of age, you notice that there are a lot of younger workers who are paid less than you who would love to jump into your position if they got the chance. For the first time in your life you entertain the prospect of doing something you might not relish doing for the next twenty years because you need the income, security and benefits of the job you have. You're afraid to take a chance and try something new.

No matter who you are or what your station in life, there comes a time when you begin to look at your life from the perspective that it is finite. You are running out of time. How are you going to utilize the time you have left?

There Is Hope

This book is for men in their forties, fifties, sixties and beyond, who want to utilize what strength and time they have left for the right purposes and in the right way–so that they will be able to say with certainty, "I have finished well."

Looking back

At some point in our lives most of us take a look back. Some might wish they could start over. Or wonder if their life would have been better "if only" they had chosen a different path…a different spouse…a different career…a different city. For others looking back is the logical consequence of an early commitment to live their lives successfully and finish well. They've spent their lives with the end game in view.

Whatever your particular circumstances, looking back is a natural and even desirable part of growing older. One scene from the Box Office hit, "Saving Private Ryan" illustrates the power and emotion of looking back:

With tears blurring his vision James Ryan, an elderly man visiting a World War II cemetery for American Soldiers in France with his family, stands in front of the cross marking the grave of Captain John H. Miller. Captain Miller died on June 13, 1944.

The movie is about a Private, who was one of four brothers. All served in the military in World War II. One died trying to take Omaha beach. Another died trying to take Utah beach.

A third died in the Pacific theater. When central command realizes that the Ryan's have lost three of their four sons, the decision is made to find the fourth son, Private Ryan, and send him home to safety and his family.

The assignment is given to Captain John H. Miller, played by Tom Hanks. He recruits seven soldiers to go with him. Private Ryan had parachuted into France just ahead of the D-Day invasion. Things went wrong and his company was scattered across a broad area held by the Germans. They eventually find him, but in the process several of the eight men lose their lives. After finding Private Ryan the captain is hit and goes down near the end of a fierce battle. When Private Ryan rushes to help, the dying Captain pulls him close and whispers in Private Ryan's ear,

"Earn this. Earn it."

Private Ryan is sent home and lives a full life raising a family. And yet, he is daily reminded of the dying words of the Captain. He knows many others gave their lives trying to save him. He never forgets Captain Miller's words–his plea for Private Ryan to live a life worthy of the sacrifices made to rescue him.

Decades later, Private Ryan is the elderly man standing in the World War II cemetery. He knows the end of his life is near. He needs reassurance that he has accomplished the mission given to him by Captain Miller. Kneeling in front of the Captain's cross in the windswept cemetery in Northern France, he sums it all up:

"Every day I think about what you said to me that day on the bridge. I've tried to live my life the best I could. I hope that was enough. I hope that at least in your eyes I've earned what all of you have done for me."

Then Ryan stands and pleadingly says to his wife,

"Tell me I've led a good life. Tell me I'm a good man."

Saving Private Ryan is a compelling story that brings home the realities of war. And although the circumstances of Private Ryan's life were unique, his feelings at the end of his life are not. When faced with the end of life, most men have the same questions.

Did I live a good life?

Did I accomplish anything of value?

Will anything I did last?

Was my life worthwhile?

Not knowing the answers, most would like some assurance. "Tell me I've led a good life. Tell me I'm a good man."

This book is about getting to the end and not having to wonder about the answers to those questions. It's about finishing life in such a manner and with such a focused purpose that you know the answers. You will know you finished well. You will have reached the end with a sense of satisfaction – not regret.

Understanding how to finish well is the journey we are about to take.

CHAPTER 2

You Were Made
To Finish Well

It's there, deep in the heart of every man. The desire to compete and win. To strive and accomplish. To get a word of encouragement that says you've done a good job.

It manifests itself at a very young age. You don't have to tell boys to think about winning. Every game in the driveway has purpose beyond the skills of the game itself. They're all about winning.

It starts in boyhood and stays there all the way into the adult world. Wherever you find men, you'll find competition. A simple round of golf becomes a tournament. One such round of golf is vivid in my memory. On the first tee we established the rules–the losers would kneel down on the ground, raise their hands to the winner and declare, "You are the greatest golfer I've ever known." Now please realize these weren't boys or teenagers. They were grown men–some with gray hair. It's a funny picture. It also beautifully illustrates the point. Men are made to compete.

Of course this innate desire is not just about winning. That's just one aspect of it. The real desire is for affirmation. We want to be recognized. To have someone tell us we've done well.

Educators know this. That's what's behind the emphasis on "building self-worth" in children. Educators want children to have good self-concepts. Why? Because they know that individuals who have good self-concepts do better in life. They are better adjusted to take on the trials and challenges of life, as well as build and nurture solid relationships. A good self-concept comes from successful accomplishments and affirmation. We are much more likely to shine when we are affirmed and encouraged rather than put down and discouraged.

The desire for affirmation is an integral part of the way God made men. He created us and put these desires in our hearts. Furthermore, God wants to fulfill those desires. Psalms

37:4 says, "Delight yourself in the Lord and he will give you the desires of your heart." Similarly, Psalms 145:19 says, "He fulfills the desires of those who fear him."

So, when we talk about finishing well, we don't have to explain why that's a good idea or a desirable goal. Every man knows inside that's the option that appeals.

The very fact that the desire is there means it was meant to be fulfilled. Think about it. The desire itself is evidence. C. S. Lewis, the British educator, theologian and writer, put forth this idea. There are examples all around you. Animals are hungry. To fulfill that desire God has provided food. The desire points to the means of fulfilling the desire. Men have a desire for love and a sexual relationship. God created male and female as the means of fulfilling that desire. In fact, if there were no fulfillment for a desire, how would we define what the desire was or what to do about fulfilling it?

Similarly, God has placed a desire in men's hearts to win, succeed and be affirmed. All through life men set goals and take on tasks with the desire to be successful and reap the recognition of having succeeded. Some of these tasks are small and of little consequence. Like taking out the garbage. Not a life or death issue, but you would still like to be recognized and thanked for having done it. Others, like putting your life on the line for freedom and democracy have huge implications. Recognition and affirmation are all the more important. And that brings us to the end of life issues. The greatest challenge in life with the possibility for the most fulfillment is in defining and taking on the task of finishing well. It is a paramount desire that God has placed in your heart. And the fact that the desire is in your heart points to the possibility of it being fulfilled.

What Does Finishing Well Look Like?

To begin it's important to realize we're not trying to define something that is attainable by only a few men. It must be something any man can accomplish. That doesn't mean everyone will. It doesn't even mean that a majority will finish well. It merely means that given the desire and a willingness to step up to the plate, it is available to all.

Our definition must be qualitative. It must be as achievable by a wheelchair-bound man as by a man with full use of this arms and legs. And since we are all going to die, and that usually means a decline in physical abilities, stamina and health in general, a good definition of finishing well qualitatively should be available throughout the final years of life as well as in the dying process.

Finishing well means discovering and accomplishing personal goals that have to do with the quality of your life. However, it's more than just achieving goals.

Many have the goal of acquiring wealth to provide a comfortable and luxurious lifestyle. The thought is that materialism increases the quality of life. However, material wealth and the kind of "quality of life" it brings have little to do with finishing well. It also isn't primarily about achieving a series of successful accomplishments or educational achievements that would be seen by most as adding to the quality of your life.

The personal goals that are critical to finishing well flow

out of your purpose.

How did you get here?

Why are you here?

What are you suppose to accomplish?

Finishing well means the ability to end your life here on earth with a profound sense of joy and peace, knowing you have led a meaningful and fulfilling life in living and achieving the goals placed before you by God.

That's a big goal—one that suggests an even bigger question:

"How can it be done?"

I like to divide life into two broad categories—the "doings" of life and the "beings" of life.

The doings are those things that have to do with activities. It's our work, recreation, the tasks we have to accomplish, and the many relational things we do. It is the "visible" side of life.

The beings are the invisible parts of life. They are all about your character and the spiritual side of life. They also have to do with personality, temperament and relationships.

Both doings and beings are important. God made us to be doers. The Bible says that in the Garden of Eden before Adam and Eve sinned, God assigned tasks for them to do. The garden was to be tended and cared for. Many people think that work came after the fall of man. As a result of sin, work was a part of the curse. Nothing could be further from the truth. Work was a part of the created order from the beginning.

Of course it is true that work became toil after the fall, but work itself was always a part of God's design. That's why most men are not happy without work being an integral part of their lives.

The doings of life are important. God implanted a desire to do things and achieve goals. Doing your job well. Going on trips. Enjoying the natural world that God created. Building your skills in whatever interests you. In a word, you want to "experience" life and all that it offers to the fullest extent possible.

However, in the final analysis the beings side of life is more important. The kind of person you are is more important than what you have done. Who you have been. What you are becoming. Your character does count. And most important the relationships you have with others and with God bring the real meaning to life. Very few men could successfully be hermits. It just doesn't fit. We were created as social beings.

The beings of life have a profound affect on the doings of life. Character is not just personal and relational. It is also important to society as a whole. Much of the functioning of our society is based on a simple level of trust. Being honest is so important a great portion of our laws are in place to protect people from the potential dishonesty of others. Government agencies are set up just to insure honesty in the marketplace. For example, we prosecute a business or an individual for false accounting.

However, character is not just important to the proper functioning of our society, it is also vitally important to you as an individual. Think back to a time you did or said something that you have since regretted. Sometimes you regret something because it has negatively affected a relationship you value. But, there are also things you deeply regret that don't really involve an important relationship. They are simply things that reflect on your character. Things you don't really want to believe about yourself.

You have been and are currently becoming the person you will be at the end of your life. And although no one is perfect or ever will be, we all strive to become more mature. More consistent in our behavior vis-à-vis what we know we should be. Deep down inside we are made to aspire to, honor and admire righteous character.

On the relationship side, most of us don't need much convincing that being with others is important. Depending upon your temperament you may be able to take a trip by yourself for a few days or even a week or two. But it's not long before you'll miss your family and friends. And think of how much more fun it is to do something or go somewhere with someone else rather than by yourself.

Developing and valuing relationships is a vital part of a fulfilling human life. The longer term the better. Shared memories, trust, knowing and counting on the character of another, confiding your innermost thoughts, desires, ambitions and fears are all a part of relationships. These beings of life set the tone, the flavor of everything else you do.

Consequently, relationships are primary, much more important than activities. However, activities are the doings around which and through which the relationships take place. We need an excuse to be together. A task or experience to share. A thought to talk about.

Of course your relationship with God is the most important relationship of all. That's the ultimate reason we were created. It's why we have a longing in our hearts for God. It's been called a "God shaped hole" that only He can fill. By far the majority of men try to fill this longing with everything but God. All sorts of other things and activities are tried, but ultimately to no avail. The hunger remains. It can only be filled when we at last take the focus off ourselves and turn our lives over to God and invite him to dwell in our hearts.

Your relationship with God is the foundation of finishing well. Without that in place everything else will ultimately ring hollow. Only as you build your doings and beings on the foundation of this relationship can you hope to look back with the satisfaction that comes with finishing well.[1]

It's Never Too Late To Finish Well

Even with your dying breath you can finish well in God's eyes. It's never too late to accept Him and begin that relationship. However, even though it is possible to turn to God late in life, it is sad to consider a life lived without God. A life lived in a way it wasn't meant to be lived. A life enormously less fulfilling.

Some think that the way to get the most out of life is to live on the fast, feel-good track for as long as you can and then in the end turn things over to God. In other words, sin is more

---

1 If you don't have a relationship with God, you can start right now. It's as simple as A-B-C.

Acknowledge that you have sinned and repent of trying to run your own life without God. Isaiah 53:6 says, "We all, like sheep, have gone astray, each of us has turned to his own way; and the Lord has laid on him the iniquity of us all." Romans 3:23 says, "..for all have sinned and fall short of the glory of God ... " Romans 6:23 says, "For the wages of sin is death, but the gift of God is eternal life in Christ Jesus our Lord."

Believe that God sent His son Jesus Christ to die for your sins and that through Christ He offers the gift of eternal life. John 3:16 says, "For God so loved the world that he gave his one and only son, that whoever believes in him shall not perish but have eternal life." In Ephesians 2:8–9 it says, "For it is by grace you have been saved, through faith–and this not from yourselves, it is the gift of God–not by works, so that no one can boast." You can't earn your salvation. It is a gift. All you have to do is accept it by asking Jesus to live in your heart.

Commit your life to Jesus Christ. Tell him you want him on the throne of your life from this day forward. Your life will begin to change immediately to become more like Jesus Christ.

A-B-C, take a moment now. Bow your head. Ask Jesus to come into your heart. Your journey toward finishing well will start on the right track. Next, grow in your relationship with Christ by reading your Bible daily and praying–start with the book of John in the New Testament. Then, find a good church home that will encourage your walk with Jesus Christ.

fun so pursue it as long as you can with gusto. To be sure, at the point of temptation, that perspective almost always appears to be the case–even when we know better.

What would be more exciting? Yielding to the lure of a beautiful temptress or walking away and saving your purity until marriage or staying faithful to your wife? At the moment yielding is far more enticing. But the price is huge. On the long haul yielding is anything but satisfying. The rewards for waiting or being faithful far surpass the momentary thrill.

One of the challenges to living and finishing well is that we are surrounded by messages enticing us to do the very things that will ultimately lead to living and finishing poorly. Take sex for example. For starters it's a drive that dominates a considerable amount of a man's thoughts and behavior throughout life. Especially in the teen and younger adult years. When used as God intended, sex brings great joy personally and fulfillment into a marriage relationship. It bonds two souls together in a way that nothing else can.

However, our sex saturated culture constantly entices us to pursue sex inappropriately. Movie after movie, sitcom after sitcom, song after song extol the pleasures of recreational sex. Rarely, if ever, do they show the consequences of such a lifestyle. Is it any wonder that sexual activity starts at an ever-younger age and the rate of out-of-wedlock births has skyrocketed?

So a big part of finishing well is to keep yourself on the right path. You have to filter all the messages coming at you through what you know to be ultimately true concerning what brings real, long-lasting joy and fulfillment.

Our goal should not only be to finish life well but to live all of life well—from beginning to end. That's the real ideal. At each stage, each season, order your life in a manner that brings the fulfillment, peace and joy you innately crave.

Although that is the ideal, we all get off track for various periods of time. The important thing is not what you have done in the past, but what you are doing right now and what you are going to do in the future. For many it would have been better if they had been faithful to their first wife and avoided the pain of divorce for them and especially their children. But that is history. The issue now is what are they doing to be faithful to their present wife?

It's never too late. In spite of regrets anyone can make the necessary decisions to finish well. Whether you are 30, 40, 50, 60, 70, 80 or older, you can make the decisions that turn your life toward the ultimate goal of finishing well. Better at 40 than 50 or 60, but whenever is better than never.

It's not about how old you are or what you have recently been doing or not doing with your life. It's what are you going to choose to do today and tomorrow that counts the most. Finishing well is there for any man who wants it.

CHAPTER 3

What Doesn't Work

It's a part of human nature to want to make your own decisions. Do what appears best at the time. Do what you want to do. Although there are countless examples from history and around us today of those behavior patterns and activities that harm rather than help, somehow we aren't convinced. It's easy to think we will be the exception. We can do as we please with impunity. We can make poor decisions without consequence.

Parents see this pattern in their children – especially during the teen years. They try to save their children the pain of learning things the hard way. More often than not, it doesn't work. It seems that the best way for a child to learn not to touch a hot stove is to touch a hot stove. Guess what? It's hot! It burns! It hurts!

And so it goes through many of the growing experiences of early life. Warnings are issued. Advice is given. And then the teen years arrive when advice is often not heeded. In fact, it's often ridiculed.

- Teenagers + automobiles = accidents. Be careful and attentive when you drive.
- Nothing much good happens after midnight.
- Premarital sex brings a lot of heartache.
- Studying for an exam will bring better results.
- Hanging out with the wrong crowd will not turn out well – select your friends carefully.
- Don't borrow money. Debt is a trap.
- Don't lie. The truth will always come out in the end.
- Character counts.

The list could go on and on. Fortunately most teens do grow up and begin to realize that their parents really were looking out for their best interests. Mark Twain probably said it best when he noted that as a young man in his teens he thought his father was fairly ignorant about the ways of the world. But, by the time he was in his early twenties he was amazed at how much his father had learned.

You would think that after the teenage experience, we would be smarter and better equipped to take advice. However, it is still our nature to want to figure it out for ourselves. In addition, there is a belief buried deep within and almost untouchable from the outside that says, "I am different. I can manage my way through this situation and come out on top, even if the statistics overwhelmingly say I will fail."

Human beings are stubborn. We steadfastly refuse to listen to others, learn from the past, or believe that statistics will apply to us. We forge ahead with a belief that "my experience will be different."

This mindset is not just prevalent in people who are in difficult situations for one reason or another. It is front and center when it comes to living a life that will bring purpose, fulfillment and lasting joy and peace. We are attracted by what we "believe" will bring us what we want. Feelings and emotions run the show.

The Old Testament book of Ecclesiastes focuses on the search for meaning and purpose in life. Solomon, one of the wealthiest men who ever lived and one of the wisest, talks about his experiences trying to find answers to his search for purpose, meaning and fulfillment. In Ecclesiastes 1:9 he said, "What has been will be again, what has been done will be done again; There is nothing new under the sun." Of course we know that is not true in the technological sense; however, it certainly is true when it comes to human nature.

I had a Sunday School teacher in junior high who said on many occasions, "Times change, but man doesn't change." How true. Think about it. If every generation learned just one thing from the previous generation about charting a more fulfilling life course, mankind would be on an upward road toward more successful living. Less conflict. More cooperation. Better understanding.

Recently mankind has progressed at a rapid rate technologically. From horses to automobiles to airplanes to spaceships. From letters to Fax's to emails to instant messaging to text messaging. From LP records to eight-track tapes to cassettes to cds to MP3. Progress everywhere. While I still think of computers as a new technology, my son and daughter have never known a time in their lives when there weren't computers. It's not new technology to them.

Now think about the behavioral side of life. Can you think of one thing that was done commonly in past years that brought poor results that is not being done today as well? The answer is unfortunately, no. From a behavioral point of view every generation, every person starts at the same place as everyone else in history–the very beginning.

Sure, we all learn as we grow to adopt many if not most of the proper social behavior patterns, like being kind or polite and saying thank you. Yet every one of us gives in to anger or rudeness or jealousy in certain circumstances. And most of us do so over and over again. Chuck Colson, former counsel to President Nixon and founder of Prison Fellowship, has possibly said it best. It's not that some people are good and others are bad, even though there are many examples of those who fall decidedly on one side or the other. The line between good and evil passes right through the center of the heart of each person. We are all capable of wonderful things and awful things.

In spite of centuries gone by, mankind collectively killed

more people in the twentieth century than in all the centuries before combined. And it was not just because of war. There was genocide on a scale that the world had never before seen. From Hitler to Stalin to Pol Pot – literally tens of millions of innocent people were slaughtered.

It's hard to look at those statistics and believe mankind is getting better or is inherently good. The fact is mankind has advanced very little, if at all, other than technologically.

So it is with our personal choices. When it comes to choosing a path to bring purpose or fulfillment to our lives, we almost always go back to where previous generations have been; believing that attainment of certain things will bring the desired and fulfilling result.

There are many paths that men eagerly pursue to bring fulfillment in life. The following are noteworthy in that they are the most tried and yet invariably never deliver the promised results:

Money

To one degree or another we all believe that more money will make us happier. And, as is true with most alluring false ideas, there is an element of truth in the belief.

If you are in debt, more money will pay off the debt and lead to a better situation and presumably a happier state. If you had more money, you could provide your family with a better standard of living. A better house. Better or more educational opportunities. Better neighborhoods. All those are true.

But, here's the rub. What you get is never enough. You always want more. Always.

People earning $40,000 per year think they would have it made if only they earned $50,000 or $60,000 per year. However, those that earn $60,000 per year believe they need to be earning $70,000 or $80,000. Even people with millions of dollars in the bank worry about having enough. It is a moving target.

If money would make you happy, then all those individuals who have money would be wildly happy. They're not! Just look around.

An overabundance of money often hurts people more than it helps. If it doesn't ruin the individual who made it, it often takes a heavy toll on the family. Children who grow up in wealthy circumstances can easily end up with poor work ethics and a sense of entitlement. Fighting over parent's wealth has divided many families.

We need enough to meet our needs and live a normal life in our communities. Beyond that money is dangerous. It can quickly lead to various kinds of pain and trouble.

Those who have the greatest peace concerning money put financial security ahead of lifestyle. They would rather have a cushion of money in the bank than live in the best house they could afford or drive the latest model car. A New York Times Best Seller, *The Millionaire Next Door* by Thomas J. Stanley and William D. Danko (1996–Pocket Books, a division of Simon & Shuster, Inc.), paints an intriguing picture of just who these people are. Interestingly enough, the most satisfied millionaires don't flaunt their wealth or have an extravagant lifestyle that would indicate great wealth. They are prodigious savers, rather than prodigious spenders. They hate debt. A telling statistic about this group is that the most popular vehicle for millionaires in the United States is a Ford F150 pickup truck—not a Lexus, Mercedes or BMW. They are truly the millionaires next door and you don't know it.

Money is an issue that affects everyone and will never go away. Too little money brings grief. Too much brings a barrage of problems and responsibilities that most of us are not equipped to handle. Money is not something that will be fulfilling in and of itself. If you will think of yourself as a steward rather than a spender, your chances of handling money well will be greatly enhanced. As will your happiness and fulfillment.

Sex

Fueled by a divinely given drive, God intended a man and a woman to join together in love to form a bond in the covenant of marriage to bring children into the world and raise them up to be responsible, loving adults. Marriage was designed with the long-term view. In giving traditional marriage vows both the bride and groom promise to love and cherish each other until death separates them. And that's not just if everything works out OK. It's a promise for better or worse, in sickness and health, and in good times or bad. In other words it is a commitment, which is the glue that forms a family and provides the stability that is best for nurturing and raising children.

In marriage a man and a woman desire to know each other intimately—body and soul. Sex is the physical side of a spiritual union.

This is the context in which God intended sexual appetites

to be fulfilled. It is also the context in which they are most meaningful and satisfying.

Our modern culture on the other hand, repeating mistakes of past cultures, has twisted the focus of this drive to pleasure without the commitment. The result is recreational sex with the focus on short-term, immediate gratification. New forms of birth control, like the pill, which arrived in the 1960's, took away the "fear" of having an unintended pregnancy. Combine that with the rejection of absolute moral standards and the "free sex–make love not war" sexual revolution began in earnest.

Television, movies and music extol the pleasures and benefits of recreational sex. Rarely are the all-to-real consequences of disease and heartache shown. The problem of pregnancy is prevented or whisked away by abortion for those who do not want to deal with the responsibility or inconvenience of children. It is so important to promote recreational sex and protect the "right" of a woman to have an abortion, that society has passed and accepted all kinds of laws that cannot stand logical scrutiny.

How can the same society say that a school cannot give first-aid treatment, often including just a band-aid, without parental permission and yet allow, and in some cases promote, a surgical procedure (abortion–a procedure that can have significant side effects) without parental notification?

Such is the absurdity and result of a sex saturated society that promotes sex as a pastime. The question you have to ask is whether all this coupling is bringing the joy and satisfaction promised? The answer is an emphatic "no!"

Infidelity almost always brings incredible pain and usually leads to divorce. The spouse always feels betrayed. If we really believed in recreational sex, why should anyone be upset? Could it be that innately we know a violation of trust has occurred? So, why are we not listening? Why can't we see that the promises of unfettered pleasures are really lies?

The sexual drive is strong enough without all the promotion. Many men fall for the lies and think if they add enough sexual pleasure to their lives they will find fulfillment. Sadly, for them and their families, the reality is that it is not true.

Free sex in abundance is not the answer. And it never will be.

Power

For some people, power is more seductive that either money or sex. After all, isn't that what the temptation was to Adam and Eve? To become Gods? Imagine having the power to do whatever you wanted.

The writers of the United States Constitution knew the danger of power and its seduction. The checks and balances they built into the structure of the government are designed specifically to check human nature. Excessive power always corrupts. We can trust no one to have power without becoming tainted by it to some degree. Our nature is to grasp more and more and to use it selfishly rather than altruistically.

Recent history brings some extreme examples of power gone ragingly wrong. Hitler, Saddam Hussein, Saddam's sons (Qusay and Uday), and Stalin. Brutal. Inhumane. Frankly, unbelievable ruthlessness. However, you don't have to go to those extremes to find power abused. Just look at local or national politics. Or your boss at work. Or the bureaucrat who makes you jump through hoops to meet regulations.

For that matter look at yourself. In one way or another, to one degree or another, haven't we all abused even the small amounts of power that we have obtained?

Fame

To be famous is another common desire. To live a life that people admire today and will also be remembered for centuries to come looks like it would be immensely fulfilling.

There's something enticing about fame, even though, from a practical standpoint, it leads to a lot less freedom in life. Who would choose to be hounded by autograph seekers? Oh, I admit that for a period of time it would be a heady experience. But after a while it would grow tiresome. You'd love to be able to go somewhere and not be recognized.

However, in spite of the downside issues, fame–along with fortune, which often go hand-in-hand–is intoxicating. We really do begin to believe the press. We soon believe we are more capable than we really are. We delude ourselves.

Several years ago I took a tour of Washington, D.C. As we drove through the city on the tour bus we saw many statues. Think about it for a minute. There's no doubt about it, you would have to have been someone pretty important to get a statue made of you to be placed in a prominent square in the nation's Capital. And yet it was amazing to me that even the tour guide often didn't know the name of the individual represented by a particular statue.

I remember clearly one particularly large statue of a horse and rider. No one seemed to remember the name of the rider or what he had accomplished. But the tour guide did know that the statue had gained a lot of public attention over the years. The horse was originally created as a stallion. Some individuals took offense that the stallion's anatomy was so visible, since it was standing tall above the crowd. So it was decided to make a "gelding" out of the stallion. The statue became known more for this change in anatomy than for the original act of honor or heroism that earned its creation in the first place.

I also remember walking the halls of the U.S. Capitol where each state is given two statues to honor two individuals who played a prominent role in that state's history. I have to admit I barely knew what the two men had done who had statues from the State of Oklahoma, where I have lived for over thirty years. And, I had never even heard of the individuals selected for most of the statues from the other forty-nine states.

(In case you're curious, Oklahoma's statues were for a Cherokee Indian named Sequoia, who created an alphabet to put the Cherokee language in writing, and Will Rogers, famous for his quick wit and good humor.)

Even for those instances where I knew what had made the individual famous, I didn't know a thing about who they really were as human beings. What were their personalities like? What about their character? Did they have a family? What was the relationship between the man and his wife or the woman and her husband? How strong was their faith and in what or who did it reside? What was their relationship to their children, if they had any?

The truth is that almost nothing of what they truly were in daily life is remembered. Only something they had accomplished or stood for is honored.

No matter how famous a person may be today, it won't take many generations (let alone years) before their memory will be all but erased. It hardly seems like a worthwhile basis for living your life.

Our short memories are not reserved just for those in the public spotlight. I attended a family reunion recently for my dad's side of the family. His father was one of thirteen children of parents who had emigrated from Sweden. Although there was a little history on the facts surrounding the age and reasons my great-grandparents came to America, very little else was known about them, except that they had thirteen children and looked fairly stern in the picture. Even my own family descendents will soon forget about the qualitative side of my life.

Of course, practically speaking, fame is an unattainable goal for virtually the entire population. Only a couple of people out of tens of millions will earn the kind of fame that will be remembered like Abraham Lincoln or George Washington.

There is a subtle but real difference to those who want to be famous for fame's sake and those who want to be remembered because they have done something significant in their lifetime. There is certainly nothing wrong with wanting to accomplish something significant. In fact, it is not usual to find at the core an altruistic desire to genuinely help others and leave society a better place.

Such proper and understandable desires may lead to leaving a name that is remembered. Nothing wrong with that. However, at the same time, never forget that your name will be associated with the thing you did, not with who you were as a person. All the valuable things mentioned above will most likely be lost and not included in the footnote that bears witness to your achievement.

Fame or leaving a name to be remembered is a poor choice to bring meaning and purpose into your life.

Of course by far the majority of us will never do anything that will either lead to fame or have a name that is remembered for accomplishing something significant. Does that mean we are free from the temptation that fame or leaving a name to be remembered will add meaning and purpose to our lives? Not at all.

Within our own circles each of us can easily be seduced by the same issue, just in another form. It's the approval of others. Wanting others to approve of what we do, even admire us, and affirm our behavior is normal. In fact it is a beneficial and necessary part of developing a good self concept. However, when raised to the wrong level of importance, it is not helpful.

Most people think that a part of their search for significance will be found in the approval of others.

Performance + other's approval = good self-esteem.

If that's the way you see life, you're playing to the wrong audience. The better way to live?

Performance + God's approval = real self-esteem.

That's playing to the right audience.

Materialism

In our western culture most of what people think will be fulfilling is summed up in our devotion to materialism and the belief that having more will bring fulfillment. If you upgrade at some point and fly first class on American Airlines, you may notice a magazine in the seat pocket with the interesting title, *Celebrated Living.*

What do you suppose is the kind of living that is celebrated in that magazine? It has nothing to do with the beings of life–the quality of character a person develops. It has everything to do with materialism and "things." Young bodies, expensive homes, cars and trips. They are all there in beautiful color. It is only too telling about what our western culture values.

It starts with children. Advertisers are in business to not just inform you about a new product or service, but primarily to making you discontent. You certainly can't be happy or fulfilled unless you have the latest and greatest. In fact, advertisers lie all the time in an attempt to entice you to buy their products. A certain hair color will make you beautiful and appealing. Clothes will make you popular. Breath mints will get the girl.

I once read an article about a man who started a game with his children, which he called "spot the lie." Every time one of the children saw a commercial that told a lie and they spotted it, he would give them a quarter. What a great way to help your children become discerning interpreters of what they are seeing!

Of course it's not just children who are targeted and hooked by slick advertising. We are all drawn by our expectations of what the next purchase will bring. You've all heard the line that the two happiest days in a boat owner's life are the day he buys the boat and the day he sells the boat. It's just one more example of how material objects never bring the fulfillment they promise.

Of course we shouldn't get carried away and pine for the rustic days of yore either. Materialism is not all bad. The operative word is "balance." Is it materialistic to want indoor plumbing when all you've ever had is an outhouse? Most would say, "Of course not!" Each newly created product or product refinement is usually based on some form of progression up from a lower level. However, the balance has to do with focus and excess. Material things will never fill the God shaped hole placed deep in every person's being. They can bring temporary comfort or a thrill. They cannot bring fulfillment and contentment, except every so briefly.

What Does Work?

If the most common goals in life—wealth, sex, power, fame and materialism—won't bring the kind of joy and lasting fulfillment that most individuals desire, what could possibly step up to take their place? We'll look at the answer to that question shortly, but first we need to take a look at the framework within which finishing well takes place.

CHAPTER 4

The Framework of Finishing Well

Although finishing well has to do with both doings and beings of life, before we look at those, it is necessary to look at the bigger picture. Issues that form the framework within which finishing well takes place. There are three major ones.

1. The Time Frame

As Rick Warren says in his best seller, *The Purpose Driven Life* (Zondervan – 2002), it's not about now. If finishing well were about this life only, the amount of time you have left would be crucial. It isn't. Long or short the amount of time you have left for you to finish well is insignificant when compared to eternity.

We were made for life, but more than that we were made for eternity. Think of a football field. Suppose that 100 yard field represents eternity. You could think of your life as represented by the first ten yards. You catch the kick off in the end zone and start up field. No matter what you do or how good you look in the first ten yards, it's only the beginning. You've got a long way to go to get to a touchdown. The first ten yards just set up the rest of the action to come. Of course eternity by definition has no end. So the football field is much, much longer.

The Bible says that we were created for eternity. "He has made everything beautiful in its time. He has also set eternity in the hearts of men." Ecclesiastes 3:11. (See also 2 Corinthians 5:1-4).

We can't imagine what God is preparing for us. "No eye has seen, no ear has heard, no mind has conceived what God has prepared for those who love him." 1 Corinthians 2:9.

Imagine trying to explain to a baby in the womb what life on the outside was like. It would be unimaginable. How could the baby understand the ability to talk, laugh and sing that would be possible outside the womb? In fact, even given our best explanations, you have to wonder if a baby would want to leave the warmth, nourishment and protection of his temporary home.

It is similar with us and eternity. We can't begin to know or understand what is there, what we will be doing, or even if it is in the same dimension that we exist in.

But, we do know that it will be glorious.

If you know Jesus Christ as your personal savior, you need not fear death. It will be a mere passage into the next thing God has planned for you. Your future will be exciting and rewarding beyond your wildest imagination.

If you begin to live your life in light of eternity, things will change. For one thing, nothing will seem nearly as important here and now. Since this life is not the goal, whatever happens here is but a passing event. Most things don't mean much ten years later, and certainly won't mean much in eternity.

However, the Bible has many references to the idea that what we do here will partially determine what happens in eternity. There will be rewards waiting for us based upon what we do here and now. "For the Son of Man is going to come in his Father's glory with his angels, and then he will reward each person according to what he has done." Matthew 16:27. (See also Matthew 19:21, Luke 6:23 and Luke 14:14.)

We are told to lay up for ourselves treasures in heaven, where moth and rust do not corrupt and thieves do not break in and steal. Matthew 6:19. This is opposed to laying up treasures here and now, where moth and rust do corrupt and thieves do break in and steal.

In other words what we do here will impact the rest of our life in eternity. Character is important. Holiness is important.

Loving one another is important. They are a part of the process of laying up treasures in heaven.

2. *Your Life Circumstances*

Each one of us faces a set of unique circumstances in life. How we got where we are is a combination of many decisions and life events. Most likely the majority of decisions were our own; however, everyone's life is full of events over which they had little or no control.

For starters each one is born into a family at a given date in time and at a specific location. It makes a difference if you were born in the inner city or a farm in Iowa, not to mention being born in another part of the world.

Imagine how different your life would be if you had been born in Tanzania? It's safe to say that almost whatever the financial situation of an individual's parents was when they were born in the United States, Canada or Western Europe the situation in Tanzania would have been poorer by multiple degrees. They most likely would not have had the opportunity to be educated beyond elementary school, if that. And the opportunities available to them for their life work would be very limited.

Many North Americans and certainly most children and teenagers have no idea how fortunate they were to have picked parents that live in North America. That fact alone opens tremendous possibilities. The freedoms available to grow and develop along a path of your own choosing and the opportunities to get an education in any one of many fields are an enormous benefit and privilege. Add to that the almost unlimited work and career opportunities from which to select, which give each person the ability to shape their lives in ways that most of the world only dreams about.

The World Bank's *World Development Report 2000/2001* says that the per capita Gross National Product in the USA (purchasing power parity) was $22,404 verses $4,914 in Bulgaria, a transition country, and $1,475 in Bangladesh, a developing country. Of course money doesn't tell the whole story. Life expectancy in high-income countries is 77.8 years. It drops steadily with level of income to only 44.2 years for the least developed countries.

As you know averages are just that–averages. Some are better off. Others are worse. When you look at these broad numbers you need to remember that within the United States individual situations are not close to being equal. Although most are very well off by the standards of the rest of the world, some are very wealthy and others live in poverty and want.

Genetics also play a major role. I didn't pick the shape of my nose, the raw mental ability I would have or how athletic my body would be. No matter how much I worked at the gym, I was never destined to have the body of Arnold Schwartzenneger or Sylvester Stalone. Oh, I could bulk up for sure, but the odds of being as proportioned are small, not to mention being as handsome.

In addition to the physical appearance issues, there are health issues as well. Some people are born with a predisposition toward certain diseases not to mention actual debilitating or limiting conditions. Although I am an exercise adherent and recognize all the values of regular exercise, I don't doubt the effect of genetics on longevity.

As some like to say, "We're all dealt a different hand of cards to play."

Then there are the many decisions you have made. Robert Frost's famous poem on two roads heading in different directions through a yellow wood makes the point better than I can.

The Road Not Taken

TWO roads diverged in a yellow wood,

And sorry I could not travel both

And be one traveler, long I stood

And looked down one as far as I could

To where it bent in the undergrowth;

Then took the other, as just as fair,

And having perhaps the better claim,

Because it was grassy and wanted wear;

Though as for that the passing there

Had worn them really about the same,

And both that morning equally lay

50

In leaves no step had trodden black.

Oh, I kept the first for another day!

Yet knowing how way leads on to way,

I doubted if I should ever come back.

I shall be telling this with a sigh

Somewhere ages and ages hence:

Two roads diverged in a wood, and I—

I took the one less traveled by,

And that has made all the difference.

We have all taken our own unique path that has led us to the point where we are today. Not always of our own choosing, but nonetheless it is the path we have traveled.

Whether you are a professional or simply worked at a normal 8 to 5 job you may have had a very successful career/ work experience. Or you may have struggled with job-loss, unemployment and severe financial trouble. On the personal side you may have had a beautiful marriage and a wonderful family or you may have suffered through a devastating divorce.

It may sound simplistic, but wherever you are is where you are. That doesn't mean that things are unchangeable, but for most people contemplating finishing well, who are past the prime of their lives, the odds of a major change in their career or circumstances is fairly small.

The life circumstances in which you find yourself will most likely determine the setting in which you will live the remainder of your life. The blessing is that it doesn't make any difference where you are, what you are doing, what your health is, or how much your bank account holds—you can still finish well. Certainly your circumstances will affect what you will be able to do with your time and determine much of your flexibility, but they won't determine if you finish well or not.

Fortunately finishing well is based on a decision you make and can be played out on almost any playing field or in any circumstance.

3. *Your Worldview*

It's something everyone has, but few pay much attention to it. However, your world view is a vital component in how you live your life and it will have a significant impact on your ability to finish well.

What is a worldview? It's how you see the world. How it came into existence. On what principles or laws it operates. Where it is going.

Your worldview also answers personal questions. How did I get here? Why am I here? Why is there so much pain and suffering in the world? Is there any way to change the world and make it better, i.e. eliminate or change evil?

For example, do you believe God created the world or was it a random event? If you believe it all came about through time and chance, you have no hope to finish well in light of eternity. Your world view is naturalistic. You are only a lump of clay that will soon lose that aspect that makes it alive. Once that's gone (in other words you die), it's all over. You'd better go for the gusto now because that's all there is.

On the other hand, if you believe that God created the world–and you–with a purpose in mind, you have a solid foundation for all sorts of things that will benefit your life here and now, as well as in eternity.

If God created, then He probably also has absolutes that He wants us to follow that will bring fulfillment. On the physical side it's easy enough to see. Take gravity. Throw something up in the air and it comes down.

How many children have jumped off a roof into a snow bank only to find the snow didn't provide the cushion they thought it would? Or maybe for you it was jumping out of a tree. Very quickly we all become believers in the law of gravity and behave accordingly.

God created many other absolutes as well. They are His laws of life. Some physical. Some relational. Some spiritual. Follow them and you'll be much happier and fulfilled. Break them and brokenness and sorrow will follow. It's inevitable because it's the way God created the world.

It's man's nature to reject God because he wants to run his own life. He wants to keep himself at the center of his world, whether at work, home or out in the community. The result of leaving God out is dysfunctional in the long run. God made us to need Him. Without Him we don't function as well or fulfill our intended purpose. Instead of increasing the quality of life, putting ourselves at the center in place of God actually reduces it.

Interestingly, even though many if not most people believe the opposite, a Biblical worldview actually elevates mankind. Everyone has purpose and value because God created them, gave them a purpose and values them.

If God is not at the center of your worldview, you can't finish well in the eternal sense. Oh yes, you can finish with lots of things. You can be wealthy. You can have friends. You can claim many achievements. But, none of these will bring ultimate satisfaction. If you've been to many funerals, you have probably noticed there is a striking difference between a funeral for someone who lived for God and someone who lived without God. Funerals for the former are filled with praise and joy and a sense of hope. Funerals without such hope are often tragic events focusing only on the achievements of the deceased and how much they will be missed.

Without God your world will be built around yourself, materialism and sensuality. All incredibly compelling, but none is ultimately able to deliver what each appears to promise. Only God can fill your God shaped hole.

On the other hand if you get your worldview from the Bible, everything in life can bring purpose and meaning. Let God's word declare His intentions and guide your life. You will be immeasurably more fulfilled and joyful. And a side benefit is that what goes on in the world will begin to make much more sense. When you understand the presence of good and evil and the struggle within everyone's heart, what you see around you is understandable.

With this framework in mind–the time frame, your circumstances and your worldview–we're ready to step into

the two great aspects of finishing well–the beings of life and
the doings of life.

PART II

The Beings of Life

CHAPTER 5

You and God

Loving God

The Bible says that we were created for God's pleasure. Not for our pleasure or our accomplishments. It's all about God. We were created to bring pleasure to Him by loving Him.

When Jesus was asked what the most important aspect of life was, he answered that the greatest commandment is to love the Lord your God with all your heart, with all your soul, and with all your mind, and the second is to love your neighbor as yourself. Matthew 22:37-39. In other words the most significant thing we do in life is to focus our life and energy on God.

Similarly, near the end of his life on earth Jesus prayed to his Father and said, `"Now this is eternal life: that they may know you, the only true God, and Jesus Christ, whom you have sent." John 17:3.

There it is in a nutshell. It's all about God and His son, Jesus Christ. The purpose of life.

With this perspective it is easy to see why the lures mentioned in Part I–money, sex, power, fame and materialism–don't bring the desired results. None of them is the reason why we were created in the first place.

Each one of us has a built-in longing for God. You may have heard the saying that we are restless until we rest in Him. The problem is that we misinterpret this longing and try to fill it with activities and pursuits that are sadly lacking. They will never be capable of meeting the need. Only God can fill that need which He has placed in each of our hearts.

Finishing well is primarily about how your relationship with God in the person of Jesus Christ grows and matures. It's about pleasing Him, not you.

The strange truth is that when you focus on God and eternity, you discover that the happiness and fulfillment you have always wanted suddenly take up residence within you. By doing and being what God intended, the by-product is a happiness, contentment and fulfillment that nothing else can touch. Jesus said that the way to find your life is to lose it. By giving up what we think is important and focusing on Jesus

Christ and His living in and through us, we begin to find life in all its abundance.

Give your life away to God and you will find it. A paradox that is true beyond your wildest hopes and dreams.

It really does make sense, when you think about it. (Here comes your worldview into play.) If you want to know the purpose of a given piece of machinery, ask the inventor the purpose for which he designed and manufactured the product. Only the creator can explain in minute detail the purpose behind the created item. So it is with you. The God who created you can tell you exactly why you were created, what He wants you to become and what He wants you to do.

Contrary to looking to God for the answer, most individuals straighten up a bit, throw back their shoulders, raise their head and agree with the lyrics of Frank Sinatra's "My Way." They think that ultimate fulfillment will come as they are able to live their lives according to their own agenda and see their desires and dreams being fulfilled.

Nothing could be further from the truth. By giving up your right to do things "your way," you will discover unbelievable joy and fulfillment by doing things "His way."

It's all about God and why he created us – to love Him and to love those he placed around us (our neighbors).

Building a Christ-like Character

If you focus on loving God and your neighbor, God is then allowed to accomplish His goals for your life. His desire is to transform you to become like Jesus Christ, His only son. Although we will never completely become like Christ in this life, it is a goal we are to strive to attain.

Scripture says that we are to be holy as God is holy. Now, holiness is clearly not our natural state. Something has to change. That change is becoming like Christ in thought and behavior.

Becoming like Christ seems both unreachable and, at times, confusing. Take a passage like the Beatitudes in Matthew 5. In verse 3 it says, "Blessed are the poor in spirit for theirs is the kingdom of heaven." Who wants to be poor in spirit? Most men would read that and respond that they want to be up-beat and go for the gusto. Your nature seems to be set against what the Beatitude promotes.

So then, how can you be changed to become like Jesus Christ? Romans 12 verse 2 gives a hint. It says we are to be transformed by the renewing of our minds.

As we turn our lives over to God, He changes our desires, our thoughts and our character–all to come into conformity with those of Jesus Christ.

The fruits of the spirit, as outlined in Galatians 5 verse 22, are "love, joy, peace, patience, kindness, goodness, faithfulness, gentleness and self-control." Wow, what a list. Traits I'd love to have.

The passage goes on to say, "Against such there is no law." Think about that statement for a moment. Why do we have laws? Laws outline what is acceptable behavior and what is not. When society doesn't want a certain behavior, a law is usually passed "against" that behavior. That's where our saying, "There ought to be a law" comes from. When something strikes us as being wrong or inappropriate, we want to legislate against it and stop it.

The fruits of the Spirit are of such a nature that there are no laws against them. In other words, no one in their right mind wants to stop those behaviors. Who would oppose kindness or gentleness or patience? These Christ-like traits are on almost everyone's wish list.

Becoming like Christ is a life-long proposition. It doesn't happen because of determination or discipline. If that were the case we all would fail miserably. None of us could stay the course. Instead, when we turn our lives over to Jesus Christ, Scripture says that he lives in us through the Holy Spirit. And the Holy Spirit gives us the power (ability) to become like Christ.

What a blessing that it is not based solely on our own ability. As the Spirit dwells within you and renews your mind, you will find yourself beginning to desire the fruits of the spirit and to want to become like Jesus Christ. At that point you are empowered to do so.

The progression takes place a step at a time. God draws you to Himself to fulfill your created purpose. You respond and ask for His presence and power. He dwells in you, and gives you the ability to make Godly decisions. He renews your mind. Then you want more of His presence, and so the growth continues.

It's true that we constantly interrupt that growth by focusing again and again on our own desires. But, for the faithful, the long-term path is certain—we will steadily grow and become like Christ.

This process does not happen in a vacuum. You can't just sit under a tree and suddenly – or even slowly – see it happening. (Although periods of quiet reflection are a good idea.)

Becoming like Christ is what happens in the process of living life. Life circumstances are the playing field God uses to bring about changes and growth in your character.

He uses difficult circumstances to teach you patience. He will have you involved with "unlovable" people to teach you how to love others. In fact, whatever He is trying to develop in you, He will bring about or allow circumstances or people into your life, which will tend to bring about just the opposite of Christ-like thought or behavior. You will want to be impatient. You will want to get even and be unkind. It's your nature.

I have a friend who likes to say that you can almost always bank on the fact that whatever your natural human response in a given situation, Jesus would have you do the opposite. Think about it. He says to love your enemies – we want to kill them. In fact, we often find it hard to love our friends and family, let alone our enemies. He tells us to look at the plank in our own eye instead of the speck in someone else's eye. Our natural tendency is to respond in anger rather than love when we are wronged. In each of those situations, only when we depend upon His power will we grow and begin to transform our natural response.

Most people long for a trouble-free life. Wouldn't it be wonderful if the end of your life were filled with peace and contentment? However, no one lives a life that is free of temptations and evil desires. In addition, evil events will surround your life. They are part and parcel of the free will that God has given and honors. It's not being tempted that is a problem; it's how you respond.

In fact I have found that the most growth in my character has come about during difficult circumstances and periods of suffering. When times are good, it is easier to cruise along and ignore God or keep Him at arms length. But when we are suffering, we turn to God and ask for comfort and help. It's been said that God whispers in your pleasure, but shouts through your pain. For this reason, don't look at suffering as something to avoid. Instead look at what God will do in you through the experience.

Before we finish this topic, I don't want you to think that finishing well is going to leave your life in turmoil right up to the end. Quite the opposite is the goal. Internally you can be content and be at peace. It's the external that you can't control.

Seeing The Unseen

As human beings it is natural to focus on what we can actually see. But there are a lot of elements of life that are unseen and are very important.

2 Corinthians 4 verse 18 says the following:

"So we fix our eyes not on what is seen, but on what is unseen. For what is seen is temporary, but what is unseen is eternal."

The real battle (the Bible calls it "spiritual warfare") occurs in our hearts and minds. We tend to look at what we can see because it's easier. It appears to be more concrete. But the unseen is what is most important.

For example, you can't "see" a person's attitudes or beliefs.

You can see how they affect his behavior, but you can't actually see them. And yet they are extremely important because they are the basis of his behavior. You can't "see" love or emotions, but you can sure see the effect they have. They are powerful and can completely change a person's actions.

Look at another example.

There are two men who have been faithful to their wives for 40 years. They both believed the vows they took the day they said, "I do." Both have lived through difficult as well as pleasant marital experiences.

However, there are differences.

One man has lusted after other women his entire life. He looks but does not touch "because he made a vow." But, emotionally he wishes he could let down his guard and have a fling now and then.

The other man truly loves his wife and knows the kind of pain infidelity would cause. Although he is occasionally tempted and drawn toward immediate gratification like any other man, he chooses not to fulfill the temptation and instead turns gratefully back to the woman he loves for true fulfillment.

On the outside (the seen) both of these men appear the same. Neither has broken his vow. Both have been faithful. But the comparison ends there. The hearts of the two are like night and day. One is living up to the letter of the law even though he would like to do differently; and the other is living up to his vow because it is what he genuinely wants to do.

This same dynamic can be found in all our lives in various different ways. How often do you do one thing when you actually feel or believe differently? You do what is expected or required, but it is not your heart. Wouldn't you want to genuinely feel compassion for the poor and disadvantaged instead of merely supporting a fund drive that you are expected to participate in? Instead of harboring hatred for someone who has committed a terrible crime, wouldn't it be better if you could genuinely pray for his soul while still holding him accountable for his actions?

What is most important in life are things that are unseen. Basically this boils down to internal character traits and relationships. They have lasting value and are permanent. Everything else is passing away.

When Scripture talks about storing up treasures in heaven, it's talking about the unseen. As you focus on God and become more like Christ you will be storing up treasures in heaven. Your character will overflow into relationships, which will be impacted for the better and for eternity.

It's not just character that counts. What's really important is Christ-like character.

Remember that everything else in the chapters to follow concerning the beings of life and the doings of life are not the main focus. They are only the playing field. *The single most important goal in finishing well is to focus on loving God and becoming like Jesus Christ.*

CHAPTER 6

Your Principles

Tom Butler is the Chairman of Teleflora, the largest flowers-by-wire company in the world. On the wall of his office is a framed, embroidered phrase that Tom has said on many occasions. In fact, he said it so many times that a florist decided to sew it for him as a memento.

The phrase is:

Don't lie, don't cheat, don't make promises you can't keep.

Not a bad standard for someone in business. Tom has orchestrated his professional life around this principle. It has served him, his associates and customers well.

Next to your spiritual foundation, your principles are often the most visible aspect of your "beings" in life. They are what you stand for. The basis upon which you make many decisions.

When you think about a strategy to finish well, your principles will be a major player in your day-to-day activities. How you treat others and how you act will flow from these principles.

Tom Butler's standard is all about integrity. The dictionary defines integrity with respect to a person's character as honesty, sincerity or uprightness. It is something that everyone should guard carefully. Yet many compromise their integrity without even thinking about it.

For example, it happens every day in the checkout line. If you are given too much change and you know it, what do you do? Do you quietly put it in your pocket–knowing the cashier will never know the difference–or do you bring it to his attention and give the money back?

If you've ever worked in a business and were responsible for processing payments, you know there are many opportunities to take advantage of mistakes.

Most invoices itemize both the balance that is due for the current month's activity as well as previous unpaid balances. The two are totaled at the bottom. It is not uncommon for payments of previous balances to arrive after the cutoff date and not show up on the current invoice. It is also not unusual for the clerk processing the current invoice for payment to go ahead and pay the total due indicated at the bottom rather than just the current amount due, because he or she doesn't check to see if payment on the previous balance was already sent.

It would be easy for the company receiving such a double payment to just keep the extra money. Many companies would never catch that they paid twice. If they realize the mistake and call for a refund all you would have to say is, "Let us check our records and we'll get back to you." Then, make a follow-up call and confirm that the double payment had been made, apologize for not catching it, and send the refund. The recipient would most likely believe your story and be grateful that you had promptly refunded the overpayment.

Such a practice could – and often does – lead to extra money on the bottom line. Even though it is dishonest, as long as you can get away with it, many wouldn't think twice about it even though it would be a clear lack of integrity.

Would they do it if they had to confess publicly to their practice? Of course not. Only because it is a secret and the chances of getting caught are very small will they go ahead and do it. The principle of personal integrity is not applied.

You've undoubtedly heard a version of the following story: *A gentleman at the bar asked the pretty young lady if she would spend the night with him for a million dollars. She immediately agreed with a smile. After a little more conversation he asked her if she would do it for half a million, and she said, "Yes, of course." As they talked and had a couple of drinks, he kept lowering the price until at $500 the young lady responded with indignation, "What kind of a lady do you think I am anyway?" He responded, "We know what you are. We're just haggling about the price."*

Your integrity should never be for sale—at any price. The woman in this story put a price tag on her integrity. It's a clear illustration of integrity for sale at a certain price. Would you be tempted to do the same? I fear most of us would cave if the price were high enough.

However, it is even more interesting that most people will sell their integrity for pennies and not even think about it. Why would anyone sacrifice their integrity over 50 cents of extra change? Isn't their integrity worth more than that?

It's a matter of principle. What are your principles? Are they for sale?

Where do principles come from?

They are taught by our parents, schools and churches. Many are taught by society at large. They form the basis of an ordered society.

One of the foundations of western civilization that, along with freedom and private property, has brought about our incredible material advancement is the rule of law. Without it our society couldn't exist. Prosperity would plummet.

Laws often set the boundaries that form the basis of many of our principles. Yet many of these principles and the obedience of laws can be like a thin veneer. The surface looks good, but it's not very thick and is easily scratched through. People will break a law or a personal principle if faced with a particularly difficult situation or, worse, if they simply feel confident they won't get caught.

Ultimately your principles should grow out of your worldview. As a follower of Jesus Christ your principles will flow from the Bible. Principles established by the Creator of life by and through which life can be experienced to the full, and the violation of which leads to failure and despair.

The Bible is loaded with principles meant to enhance your life. The Ten Commandments are foundational (Exodus 20). They are the basis upon which all other principles grow. That's why Moses, holding tablets containing the Ten Commandments, is pictured on the back wall of the United States Senate and above the Supreme Court. In fact, in the Supreme Court Moses stands at the middle with all the other historical law figures looking toward him. The Ten Commandments were clearly seen as central to establishing the law of the United States.

Some of the Ten Commandments appear to be common sense, while others keep you on the right path and protect you from following belief systems which will lead you astray from the way God intended you to live.

- Don't put anything in the place of God.
- Don't create any idols that you worship.
- Don't misuse God's name.
- Keep Sunday holy (work six days and rest the seventh).
- Honor your father and mother.
- Don't murder anyone.
- Don't commit adultery.
- Don't steal.
- Don't lie.
- Don't covet anything your neighbor has.

In addition to the Ten Commandments there are many other

life principles found in the Bible. Solomon, the wisest man that ever lived, set down many principles in the book of Proverbs. And, then there are the many New Testament books, in addition to the Gospels, that deal specifically with how we should live a life that is devoted to Jesus Christ.

WWJD

"What would Jesus do?"

It's a great question that we often pose to young people when they are confronted with a behavioral decision. But, this standard is not just for kids and teens. It can help anyone think through their action or response in a given situation. After you have read and studied what Jesus taught and how He lived, you have a wealth of knowledge to apply to your own life.

Although the "WWJD" has been commercialized in recent years, it is a very valuable tool to help guide your thoughts and decision-making processes.

Many years ago I was given a challenge to discover the main principles Jesus taught his disciples. I was told to get a red letter edition of the Bible. In this edition all the words spoken by Jesus are printed in red so they are easy to spot. Most of the red portions are found in the four Gospels—Matthew, Mark, Luke and John, however, there are a few other instances in Acts, Corinthians and Revelation.

As I read through all the red-letter passages, I was told to pay particular attention to any principle which Jesus specifically told his disciples. These twelve men were close to Him and actually traveled with Him on a daily basis. Jesus spent three years "discipling" (teaching) them how He wanted them to live. The instructions he taught these men were essential to the principles Jesus wanted to leave behind.

I discovered ten core principles of the way He wants us to live our lives. Although you might want to group and categorize the principles differently, I believe Jesus called us to be men whose lives reflect the following characteristics.

1. A man of love

The last significant teaching Jesus gave to his disciples occurred at the last supper before the crucifixion. A major emphasis was on love. In John 13:34-35 he said, "A new commandment I give you: Love one another. As I have loved you, so you must love one another. By this all men will know that you are my disciples, if you love one another."

Two chapters later – still at the last supper – he returns to the theme of love in John 15:9-17. Just as God the father has loved Jesus and Jesus has loved the disciples, we are to love each other. Jesus wants you to be a man of love.

2. A man of the word

At first pass most would think this means to be a person who immerses himself in the Bible. However, that's a rather limited view of what the "word" is. In John 1:1 we are told that term "word" is applied to Jesus. He is the word. You might think of it in the following way: Jesus is the "living word." The things He said are the "spoken word." And the portion of his sayings, instructions and parables that are included in Scripture are the "written word."

A man of the word focuses on Jesus the giver of life – not

just the Bible. Jesus said in John 5:39-40 "You diligently study the Scriptures because you think that by them you possess eternal life. These are the Scriptures that testify about me, yet you refuse to come to me to have life." In other words, it's not just knowing what the Bible has to say. It's following the author–Jesus himself.

3. *A man of prayer*

In Matthew 6:9-13 Jesus taught his disciples how to pray. It's what we now call the Lord's Prayer. "Our Father in heaven, hallowed be your name, your kingdom come, your will be done on earth as it is in heaven. Give us today our daily bread. Forgive us our debts (sins) as we also have forgiven our debtors (those that sin against us). And lead us not into temptation, but deliver us from the evil one."

Daily prayer is a time of communion with God. Talking to God. But, it's also about being quiet and listening to what God is telling you in your heart. The Bible says we should pray without ceasing, i.e. constantly. No matter what you are doing, do it as if Jesus is there with you (he is). Do it for him. Talk to him as you feel the need and listen for his response.

4. *A man of unity*

People are attracted to unity like bugs to light. As men we naturally like to think that the winning team on the field is unified in the locker room. Jesus knew the importance of unity. In John 17:20-23 He prays that we will be in unified just as he is in unified with his father. That's the model. Jesus does what his father does and is in constant communion with him. And we know that where men are united their impact is exponential. Just as Jesus wants us to love one another, he wants us unified.

5. God before others

Matthew 22:36-37 is the greatest commandment. "Love the Lord your God with all your heart, soul and mind." That's the number one principle. God is first. Following him is more important than anything else you can do. This is the common purpose of all believers – to love God. We are to love him more than anything or anyone else. Not your spouse, your children, or your mother or father should come before God.

6. God before self

In Matthew 10:37-39 Jesus put forth a paradox that seems against all our natural inclinations, but nonetheless is true. If you will lose your life, then you'll find it. Life doesn't come from narcissistic self service; it comes from serving God and others. Do that and life will flow out of you. Matthew 16:24-26 "Then Jesus said to his disciples, 'If anyone would come after me, he must deny himself and take up his cross and follow me. For whoever wants to save his life will lose it, but whoever loses his life for me will find it.'"

7. A man who bears good fruit

In Matthew 7:15-20 Jesus says that men are known by their fruit – just like the clothes we wear. Good trees bear good fruit and bad trees bear bad fruit. We have lots of similar sayings, such as "You will reap what you sow" or "Tiger's don't change their stripes." What/who you are will be evident by the results of your life–your fruit.

In John 15:4-5 Jesus said, "Remain in me, and I will remain in you. No branch can bear fruit by itself; it must remain in the vine. Neither can you bear fruit unless you remain in me. I am the vine; you are the branches. If a man remains in me and I in him, he will bear much fruit; apart from me you can do nothing."

8. A man who puts God before possessions

It's a natural tendency for men to put their trust in their possessions or bank accounts. As personal wealth increases, we trust more in our wealth and get more security from our bank account than God. But in Luke 12:15 Jesus said, "Watch out! Be on your guard against all kinds of greed; a man's life does not consist in the abundance of his possessions."

Jesus' parable of the soils (or seeds) in Mark 4 makes a similar point. In verses 18 and 19 he describes one inadequate soil this way. "Still others, like seed sown among thorns, hear the word; but the worries of this life, the deceitfulness of wealth and the desire for other things come and choke the word, making it unfruitful." Desires for possessions and wealth can get in the way of God.

In Matthew 6:25-34 Jesus said to seek first the kingdom of God and then all the other things will be added. God must be first in our lives. Even at the cost of giving up things or wealth. True wealth is found in our relationship with him.

9. A man of the great commission

The great commission is found in Matthew 28:18-20. "And Jesus came up and spoke to them, saying, 'All authority is given to me in heaven and on earth. Go therefore and make disciples of all the nations, baptizing them in the name of the Father and the Son and the Holy Spirit, teaching them to observe all that I commanded you, and lo, I am with you always, even to the end of the age.'"

However, the focus should not be on "going" and "spreading the Gospel." It should be on being with Christ–not the task. People are drawn to Christ when we show love toward one another (John 13:34-35). Through unity men are drawn to God (John 17:20-23). The great example is found in Acts 2:42. "As the disciples were together GOD ADDED (emphasis added) to their numbers daily." Why this focus on the great commission? We must live what we preach. A vibrant relationship with Christ will draw people far more effectively than our human words ever could. In a similar way you don't usually get married to have children. They are the fruit of the love and relationship between the man and the wife. So it is with Christ. Love him and the fruit will follow.

10. A man of truth

John 8:32 says "Then you will know the truth, and the truth will set you free." God loves truth. He hates lies and deceit. He loves to shine the light of day on everything so that it can be seen clearly. Don't do anything that you wouldn't want the light of day to shine on. Men love darkness because their deeds are evil. We must stand for truth and light. Truth, told in love, will always – ultimately – set men free.

These principles of Jesus should become the guidelines of how you live your life. Without them it is impossible to finish well.

Remember that the most important part of the "beings" of a life that is finishing well is to love God with all your heart, soul, mind and strength. It's all about God.

In living your life for God and in the process becoming like Jesus Christ, your principles will be very important. Not to mention, it makes living your life much easier when you become a *principled* person, who is non-negotiable on the core principles of your life.

Practical Principles

To help you stay on track, you must always keep your core principles front and center in your mind and heart. Your core principles are the fountain from which your personal, practical principles flow. Rules you live by. Your personal list of do's and don'ts. It is a good idea to write down your practical principles in your own words. Determine that these will be your "non-negotiables."

Setting limits and boundaries in advance is always good idea. Your principles will form the basis for your boundaries and limits.

For example, I don't have to think twice about giving incorrect change back to the cashier because I have determined that I always will. It's not up to negotiation. (Of course I am tempted to go against this principle almost every time it happens. But that's exactly when my predetermined behavior wins the day.) In spite of following the temptation to walk silently away, I remind myself to do what I know is right.

The same idea applies when it comes to another area where temptation seems ever present to men. Your sex life. You can save yourself a lot of heartache if you will just determine in advance what you will do and not do sexually. It is far easier to do what you know you should if you've decided your behavior and response ahead of time rather than wait to make a boundary decision in the heat (passion) of the moment.

Here is a practical example.

Men who travel alone on business often find it easy to succumb to the temptation of pornography. Magazines are readily available in most hotel gift shops. The traveler is anonymous—no one knows him from the man-in-the-moon. It's easy to succumb to a temptation that under normal circumstances in their home town would be dismissed. By establishing a personal principle that they will never purchase or pick up a pornographic magazine or watch a movie in their room that was sexually questionable, living a morally pure life on the road becomes much easier. The course of action is already laid out before the temptation presents itself.

This same kind of protection will work in every other area of your life where you might be tempted to take the wrong path. Know your principles. Set your limits and boundaries. Keep them non-negotiable.

Developing your own list of personal principles may seem like a daunting task. However, it is not as challenging as it might seem at first glance. Once you get into it, you should find compiling the list fairly straight-forward.

The list can be short or long to fit your personality; however, you might want to divide it into the major areas of your life. By breaking down the list into categories, it is easier to organize your thoughts.

Following is a listing of my principles to give you an idea of what your list might look like:

Finances

- I will live under my income.

- I will work to be debt free.
  [Being debt free is the key element in financial freedom. Although there are many good books on how to do this, here's a quick summary. First live under your income. Then work to pay off your credit card debt. Don't use credit cards again until you can discipline yourself to pay off the entire balance each month. (Hint: you will always spend less if you use cash instead of credit cards.) Next tackle other consumer loans. Then pay off your automobile. Finally get your mortgage paid off. You can do this much faster than you might think. Once your credit card debts are paid off, don't change your life style. Take the entire amount you were paying on your credit cards and apply it as an extra payment each month to your auto loan. Once the car is paid off, do the same with your mortgage. Make additional mortgage payments with the money you had been spending on paying your credit card debt and auto debt. Most couples can be completely out of debt, including their home mortgage, in five to ten years by following these steps.]

- I will always give a tithe (10%) to God's work. Some of this goes to my church and the remainder to other Christian work such as Young Life, the John 3:16 Mission, other needy Christian causes, and even non-taxable gifts to meet individual needs that I come across.

- Relationships are more important than lifestyle. I will not become a workaholic just to provide "things" for my family. Together with my wife we will determine priorities in our family life and balance our finances against those priorities.

- I will strive to make my lifestyle a "non-issue" with those I am around. In other words, I won't drive a car that most would feel is ostentatious. If the average car being driven by those in my church is a Honda or Camry, that's the amount I will spend on a car. The same principle holds true with clothes and other material possessions.

Sex life

- I will remain faithful to my wife sexually both physically and emotionally. (Although temptation is always present, I try to avoid dwelling on it.)

- I will not seek out pornography. If it presents itself, I will immediately turn away.

- I will not expose myself to sexually explicit movies or literature. I will to choose to not see a #1 rated movie rather than expose myself to temptation.

- I will not seek to be alone with women other than my wife.

Although I know I may occasionally be alone with a woman for business purposes – for example a lunch meeting – I will not seek out such encounters and I will keep the utmost in proper conduct if I find myself in such a situation. I will always opt, if possible, to include a third party if such a situation arises.

Family

- Second to God, immediate family relationships take priority over other relationships.

- My relationship with my spouse comes before my relationship with my children,

- I recognize that in my family's eyes there is no difference between quality time and quantity time. I must spend time with my spouse and children.

Work

- I will not steal from my employer. This means long distance telephone calls, office supplies or over-spending on an expense account.

- I will do my work as unto the Lord.

- I will not compromise my beliefs for advancement at the job.

- I will not intentionally harm someone else to get ahead.

- Truth and honesty will be my guidelines.

Relationships
- Other relationships will not supersede family relationships.

- I recognize the need to have a small group of like-minded men (2-4) with whom I can share my struggles and be accountable to. They must first and foremost be followers of Jesus Christ. Then they must individually be committed to my growth in and walk with Christ. If I don't have such a group, I will pray until, under the leadership of the Lord, one is formed. These men will be advocates for Christ in my life and advocates for my spouse and children.

- I will not have relationships ("friendships") with individuals of the opposite sex outside of a group context or outside of a combined relationship with their spouse as well, i.e. as a couple.

Spiritual Life
- My ultimate goal is to love God with all my heart, soul and mind.

- I will "re-up" every day to commit my life to glorifying God. I recognize that I cannot make a once and for all decision that will insure my daily life is focused on God. My self always reasserts itself on a daily basis and I must put it in subjection each day to my relationship with God.

- I will pray when I first wake up each morning thanking God and asking for guidance for the day. I will continue to pray as I go through the day for people and events that come into my life.

CHAPTER 7

How You Think

Another aspect of your "beings" of life is how you think. As you navigate your way through each day, how you think will often determine how you act. The thought always precedes the action. And, the way you think flows out of your worldview.

It's like wearing sunglasses. Everything you see is changed somewhat by the shade of the sunglasses. Some colors allow you to see things you otherwise couldn't. If you're a skier, you know that ski-goggles come with a variety of lens colors. Snow reflects light, so it is often helpful to have a darker lens to tone the light down a bit. However, there are conditions when the light is not as good, such as at the end of the day when the sun has gone down behind the mountain. It is difficult to see the moguls (bumps) well enough to ski safely. Under those circumstances a yellow or pink lens can allow you to see much better.

How you think is the same. It will set the framework for interpreting what is happening around you.

The world of competitive athletics gives further insight into the mind's power to influence behavior and performance. It's no mystery that a good portion of athletic performance comes from the mind.

Have you ever been at a football game where the momentum is favoring one team over the other? Everything they do seems to work. The other team can't stop their opponent's progress. Then something dramatic happens—perhaps an interception is made or a fumble recovered just before a touchdown. All of sudden the momentum shifts. The team that was headed for certain defeat comes back.

What's changed? Nothing physically. The same players are on the field. Same skills. Same abilities. But their perception has changed. The players are thinking differently than they did a moment before. Instead of believing they were headed for certain defeat, the once losing team now believes it can win. And the team that was previously about to score has lost some of its confidence. In each case performance changes ever so slightly—just enough to alter the outcome of the game.

It's a perfect example of how much the mind influences behavior. The mind is an amazing thing. When you think you can win, more often than not you do. When you think you can't win, most likely you won't. Your skills haven't changed.

Your muscles are just as strong. Your reflexes the same. But something from the mind makes them stronger, quicker, more coordinated.

The same is true when it comes to living your life. How you think is critically important. Correct thoughts can keep you on the right path and headed toward your goals.

When it comes to finishing well, how you think about things is important. Are you viewing the world as one in which God is ultimately in charge and you are serving Him? Do the glasses you are wearing give you a true picture? Here are just a few thought "glasses" you should have on.

Think God
"In the beginning God ... "

These are the first four words in the Bible (Genesis 1:1). It's all about God. The book of John starts by talking about Jesus being present at the beginning with God the Father. In fact, it says Jesus made (created) all things. That's *everything*. Not just a few things, but everything.

As you go through your day you need to look at everything from God's perspective. How He would have you think and behave. When you see suffering, imagine how it must break God's heart. When you see rejoicing, think how God feels when His children are so happy.

When analyzing a possible business deal or making a difficult ethical decision, think about what God would want you to do. What would be the ethical thing to do? What would bring glory to God?

When you are in midst of a relational conflict, think how God would want you to show love, concern and compassion for this person. Sometimes that might mean "tough-love". But more often than not it means putting the other person's needs ahead of yours.

When you make decisions for your kids, think what would be best to encourage their own relationship with Jesus Christ. For example, when looking at college options, don't just talk about the "best" schools academically. Talk about which choice they think would be the best for improving their relationship with Jesus Christ. After all, you want them to finish well too.

Think Eternity

Always look at life through the lens of eternity. How important will the issue you are dealing with be in a hundred years? Will it impact someone's eternal destiny?

This kind of thinking will take a lot of stress out of your life. No decision, no problem seems quite so critical in light of eternity. Your perspective is better, more balanced.

Many New Testament passages speak about receiving rewards in heaven for what we do on earth. In Matthew 16:27 Jesus says, "For the Son of Man is going to come in his Father's glory with his angels, and then *he will reward each person according to what he has done.*" (emphasis added)

How often do you think that some things you do today will earn rewards in heaven? If you do, it will have a dramatic impact on how you live. You will begin to live for eternity instead of today. A person who finishes well is a person who is living for eternity.

Think small—one on one

Most of what is accomplished in the world as far as changing someone's life happens in a one-on-one relationship. You will have more impact on your world and the future by having fewer, deeper relationships than you will by having many more shallow ones.

It's often alluring to think about being famous and to imagine the impact you could have. However, very few have that kind of fame. Of those that are famous very few have much of an impact outside of their own small circles of close friends.

Relationships in life fit nicely into a funnel. At the top of the funnel you may have many acquaintances – people who you only know socially or casually through work or activities. Down lower in the funnel are those you have had the opportunity to spend extra time with. You know them better and you know more about them. You have fewer of these relationships than your acquaintances at the top of the funnel.

As you approach the bottom of your funnel, there are only a handful of people that you can really be intimate with. They are the ones on whom you will have the most influence. Those relationships are the most important. It's where you need to primarily focus your attention. Don't trade in time with your important relationships for less important activities.

Think Big – God

Whatever you are doing, if you're doing it for God, the results can be far greater than you might imagine. When you give your talents and skills back to Him, he can multiply them many fold. In the physical world it's called "leverage." You are able to do something because of leverage that would be impossible without it. For example, take a bolt cutter. You can easily cut a bolt or a padlock because of the leverage built into the cutter. Without that leverage it would be impossible to perform the task.

Remember the story of Gideon. God's plan was to defeat the Midianites and use Gideon in the process. In Judges chapter 7 the story is told. Gideon first gathered 32,000 men to fight … but God said that it was too many. Gideon told the men that anyone who was fearful could go home. Some 22,000 did, leaving him with only 10,000 … but God said that was still too many. You see God wanted there to be no doubt in anyone's mind who had won the battle. He wanted it to be obvious that Gideon's army could certainly not have succeeded without Him. So, next God told Gideon to take his men down to the water to drink. Anyone who set down his weapons to drink was sent home … leaving only 300 men to fight. Gideon gave each man a trumpet and a torch. On his signal in the middle of the night after surrounding the Midianites, all 300 men blew their trumpets and held their torches high. The Midianites were so scared they attacked each other and wiped themselves out. God can do amazing things with the ordinary.

A similar story of Jesus feeding 5000 people further illustrates the principle. No one present had any food except a little boy who had a few loaves and fishes. But when he gave them to Jesus, who broke them and prayed, there was enough to feed everyone with food left over.

It's not primarily about what you can do with your talent. Instead, it is what God may choose to do with your talent. Leave it up to God, and don't be surprised when the results are greater than you had dared to hope. And when that happens, you'll have a new sense of how God is working in and through your life.

Think endurance

Many people see life as the pursuit of a long-sought objective. When they succeed in business, life will be good. Or, when they retire, life will become everything that they hope for.

It's not true. Don't believe it.

Life is not a destination–it's a journey. It's not a short sprint around the track once–it's a marathon. It takes endurance. You need to pace yourself.

God uses many parts of the journey to test and mold our character. Remember, in order to bring about the traits He wants in your life, He uses circumstances that tempt you to do just the opposite. You won't develop patience until you are forced to be patient. You won't develop honesty until you are tempted to be dishonest or have been treated dishonestly and see the consequences. You may not develop truthfulness until you lie and are no longer believed.

When I was young I thought that by the time I was 50 I would pretty much have figured out the big issues of life. However, ask anyone who is 60 and they will tell you that they faced many slip-ups, temptations, errors of judgment, and bouts of anger in the previous decade. Don't expect the challenges and learning to ever end. Life will always throw curveballs and challenge you. You need endurance to finish well. The good news is that the more you learn, the better you are able to face those challenges.

Every day is a new day in which you must choose to "re-up" to the task of finishing well. Every day! From now until you are ushered into His presence.

Don't think of endurance negatively, like you're out of breath and don't know if you'll make it to the finish line. Rather think of the endurance of a conditioned athlete running a race at a pace he can sustain. God gives you the same kind of strength through the power of the Holy Spirit living within you. You have the ability to see your way through any situation through His power.

Think treasure in heaven

How can you behave in a given situation that will store up treasures for you in heaven rather than here on earth? That's really where we want our savings account to be.

Jesus said, "You cannot serve God and money." Matthew 6:24. Notice the word "cannot." He didn't say, "It's difficult to serve God and money." He said that you *cannot.*

The problem is that most of us look for security in our bank account or assets. That's understandable. Lack of money usually causes severe stress. So, how can a person not serve money to some extent?

It isn't that money is evil and we should avoid it. It's not money that is the root of all evil; it is the *love* of money that is the root of all evil. Money's ok. Wealth is ok. It's just is not where our main focus should be. Our security is to be Jesus Christ. He is permanent, while nothing else in the world is. And thankfully, he has promised to provide for our needs.

This is a very difficult concept for most men. Embedded deep in our psyche is the idea that money is important. It is hard to put it into perspective. I don't believe anyone can totally solve this problem once and for all. It takes a conscious decision everyday to focus on serving God and not money. You must constantly examine your motives. You must see all of your possessions as belonging to God. You have merely been entrusted to be a steward over them. Manage your assets and possessions for God. Don't let them manage you.

Always try to evaluate your thoughts and actions in light of storing treasures in heaven not building bigger banks accounts here on earth.

Think Abiding

Jesus wants us to "rest" in Him.

Abiding has the sense of "continually" being in the presence of Jesus Christ. Many can remember when their mother said that even though she might not see everything they did, Jesus would. And this is the way many see Jesus' presence. It's like a watchdog that catches you when you do wrong and growls at you to keep you on the straight path. That's not the idea here. Jesus wants to be with you as a companion and encourager. Think of him like having your best friend with you. Someone who enhances every experience and loves you unconditionally.

We are to approach each day with the idea that we are going to go through that day hand in hand with Jesus. He should always be present in our hearts and thoughts.

Think John 10:10

Finally, remember that Jesus said that He came to give life, and give it abundantly.

Many think of Jesus as a spoilsport. He wants to take all the fun out of life. Nothing could be further from the truth. He wants to put all the real fun back into life. He wants to make it an adventure, with you seeking to fulfill His desires and His causes.

Remember God created you. He knows your purpose and how to maximize each experience. He knows what abundant life is really about. His ways and His paths will bring about an abundant life beyond your expectations. Think the "abundant life" as you traverse each day.

When you visualize abundant living, you naturally think in terms of the "doings" of life – the field on which life is played out. And that's what we turn to next in Part III.

PART III

The Doings of Life

CHAPTER 8

The Playing Field

God created you to be active. You are not just your mind. You weren't created to just sit and contemplate.

You are a physical being with arms and legs, hands and feet, eyes, ears and a nose. You eat, drink and breathe to stay alive. You have five senses—sight, sound, smell, touch and taste. You get pleasure from these senses and your physical body.

God never intended for the beings of your life to be all there is.

In fact, just the opposite, He created you such that you can't really experience the beings of life without the physical "doings."

Imagine someone telling you to grow and become like Jesus Christ by merely sitting under a tree. It would never happen. You become Christ like as you are involved with activities and people that force you to respond and grow in the midst of everyday life.

Two people who love each other can gaze into each other's eyes for a while, but soon they will get restless. What they really need to do is share life together with all its experiences. Have a common vision (beings). Walk together hand-in-hand (doings).

Think of life like a game. What God is doing in your life takes place on a playing field. That's where the action is. There are rules, goals and other players.

Your playing field is comprised of the environment in which you live and work. The players are all those you come into contact with. The rules are set by God and are under His authority.

In the process of living your "doings" will progress through many stages. Stages that change with your season of life. To better understand this process, I'd like to introduce you to Dave Jewitt, a spiritual/life coach who has particular insight into the phases of life. He has helped many men focus their lives through his ministry called *Your One Degree*.

Dave has put together a simple chart that gives insight on what most men will face during different seasons of their life. It is reproduced on the next two pages. A quick review will show you how the doings and beings of your life interact and evolve over time.

(For more information on Dave Jewitt and *Your One Degree* see www.youronedegree.com.)

Perspective Chart

	Twenties	Thirties-Mid Forties
Theme	Learning to Impact	Increasing Impact
Pressures/Concerns	Gain Knowledge	Apply Knowledge
	Initial Success	Continued Success
	New Responsibility	More Responsibility
	Dating/Marriage	Marriage partnership
	Training Children	Preparing Children
Key Question	Who am I?	What's my purpose?
Characteristics	High activity level	Intense schedule
	Broad learning	Narrowed learning
	Several Friends	Losing touch w/friends
	Hopeful/Anxious	Stressed/Tired
	Uncertain about self	Dealing with "baggage"
	Trying to find niche	Trying to get ahead
	Starting to produce	Productive
	Accomplishing	Achieving
Dangers	Faulty major decision	Purposeless busyness
Needs	Self-understanding	Life compass
	Belonging	Stability
	Guidance	Perspective
	Mentors	Mentors/Models
	Challenging friends	Close friends

Perspective Chart

	Mid Forties-Fifties	Sixties +
Theme	Broadening impact	Maximizing impact
Pressures/Concerns	Question knowledge	Using knowledge
	Mortality/Reality	Health
	Changing responsibility	Less responsibility
	Marriage closeness	Marriage friendship
	Launching children	Relating to children
Key Question	Where do I focus?	How do I finish well?
Characteristics	Changing schedule	Looser schedule
	Targeted learning	Enjoyable learning
	Few close friends	More friends
	Confused/weary	Anxious
	Questioning	Accepting
	Trying to keep up	Trying to stay useful
	Productive	Changing productivity
	Contributing	Influencing
Dangers	Plateauing/grasping	Giving up/coasting
Needs	Pacing/Focusing	Encouragement
	Adjusting	Inspiration
	Vision	Passion/heart
	Mentors/Mentorees	Mentorees
	Committed friends	Caring friends

Qualitative doings

Life is full of activity. In fact, our activities often seem to run our lives – sometimes by choice (the hobbies and activities we enjoy) and at other times out of necessity (the activity/time requirements to hold down a job).

It is easy to see how the beings of life are intimately connected to the doings of life. They are like two sides of a coin – each different, but a part of the same whole.

The doings of life can be divided nicely into two camps – qualitative and quantitative.

Qualitative doings have to do with community and relationships – marriage/family, fellow believers/church, close-friends/acquaintances. For most men life would lose its meaning and luster without relationships. Very few individuals are constituted to live the life of a hermit. We need people in our lives. Genesis 2 verse 18 sets the stage.

The Lord God said, "It is not good for the man to be alone. I will make a helper suitable for him."

There it is in a nut shell. Right from the mouth of the creator. It's not good for you to be alone. The context concerned creating a spouse for Adam, but the principle is broader than that. The necessity of relationships is grounded in how we were created. It's almost always more fun and meaningful to do something with someone else. These relationships are a significant part of the qualitative side of doings.

Of necessity finishing well means the primary focus is on qualitative doings. Those doings that build relationships are much more valuable than other activities.

To be specific, finishing well means that you want to finish well with your spouse, if you are married. You also want to build close relationships–as much as possible with your children. Then there are your co-workers that you spend more time with than your family members. Your relationships at work are no small part of the qualitative aspect of your doings. A large part of your legacy should be the relationships you build and the values and beliefs you help instill through those times together.

In addition to your biological family, you also are a member of the family of God. A significant part of finishing well is being an active member of this spiritual family. Scripture is clear that we are to love and care for other believers. John 13:35 says that the way the world knows that we are disciples of Christ is by how we love each other. Your unique talents and abilities (which we will address in the next chapter) enable you to serve others in ways that others can't because their talents and abilities are different. In I Corinthians 12 starting with verse 12 the Apostle Paul compares the relationships we have with fellow believers to the physical body. It is made up of many parts, but forms one unit. The body functions well when all the parts are working properly. Similarly, when everyone brings their particular strengths and talents to bear, our spiritual family operates well and everyone is supported.

Finally, close friends become increasingly important as you move through the seasons of life. Everyone should have a few very close friends with whom they can be totally open and honest. Usually this boils down to a small group of 2 to 4, or so, friends. Friends who share your successes, failures, concerns, hopes, doubts, beliefs and dreams. These close friends should be able to ask you the tough questions, like–how is your relationship with your spouse? Or, what are you doing that you don't want anyone to know about? (This group of necessity needs to be small, because you can't share deeply or maintain confidentiality with a large group.)

If you are going to finish well, you need a small group to whom you are accountable to help you stay the course when the path is rough. These close friends will provide the encouragement, help and the praise you need to live the life that leads step-by-step to finishing well.

Our American culture does not promote these kinds of relationships–especially among men. The hero is more often painted as one who, like the cowboy of old, rides in to save the day and then rides out alone–needing no one. Unfortunately, consistent with this image, many men go through life having only superficial relationships. They never get the few friends that they can share deeply with without fear of being rejected.

One reason these relationships can be missed is that they take commitment. Like all relationships there will be times when they are stretched and it seems like the best option is to "chuck 'em" and move along to new ones. But it's only when you stay the course and stay committed that those intimate friendships really blossom.

There are a couple of practical things you must do if you are going to succeed with these close relationships. First, you must agree to absolute confidentiality. What is shared is not told to someone else without permission. Your friend needs to know and believe that he can trust you if he is going to be willing to share his soul. Second, you need to keep short accounts. When you have a conflict, bring it out in the open and deal with it until you have a resolution. Don't sweep anything under the rug. It'll just stay there waiting for a future time to reappear and make havoc.

Quantitative doings

Quantitative doings are the "stuff" of your daily existence—sky diving, fishing, driving to work, exercising, and all the other activities that make up your day. They are an integral part of your everyday life. They bring excitement, enjoyment and fulfillment.

One key to finishing well is to make sure that you are not just doing activities for the sake of doing activities. Put purpose behind them. Don't just go fishing. Take someone with you and build a relationship. And remember to consciously take Christ with you wherever you go and whatever you do. Use the doing activity as an excuse for enhancing the beings of your life. Add meaning to activities and they'll become even more rewarding.

CHAPTER 9

You Are Unique

A significant part of finishing well is to know who you are. What talents and abilities has God given you?

The Bible says in Romans 12 verses 3–8 that you should not think more highly of yourself than is warranted. Most people do just the opposite. God wants you to take a sober look at yourself–know your strengths and weaknesses. Just like a body has many members and each member has a separate task, so it is with us. No one can do everything well. Even very talented people need to specialize if they are going to truly utilize their abilities to their highest level.

Knowing yourself is not as easy as it may appear. For most men it is a discovery process that takes time and reflection. Some even take tests or find counselors who specialize in helping people discover more about themselves. Another less expensive route, and often quite enlightening, is to ask your spouse and close friends. They probably know you better in many respects than you know yourself.

When you know who you are, you can determine the most effective place to work and serve. You can select those areas that fit your personality. Those areas, that bring you pleasure.

Every man wants to be successful. Initially most men view success in terms of their career or making money. As they get older or go deeper in their faith, they broaden the concept of "success" to include the spiritual and relational aspects of their life. So, in the end you are looking at success in several areas of your life.

Although success starts by knowing what you are good at, it is greatly aided by knowing those areas you should say "no" to. People who are the most effective have usually developed the ability to turn down requests and activities probably more often than they accept them.

Although many people think God will ask them to do something they really don't want to do, the opposite is usually the case. The needs and opportunities which God presents to you will match up with the greatest gifts and talents He has given you. These gifts and talents will become the basis of your ministry. God will always give you the abilities and resources to do what He asks you to do.

Start by "knowing what you're good at." Take a simple task like balancing a checkbook. For some people it is a major chore. For others it is simple and easy. Where you land on balancing a checkbook is largely a matter of gifts. If you've been gifted with mathematical ability, the checkbook routine is probably just that—routine.

Interestingly enough, usually those areas that are easy for you, that you can do "with your eyes closed," so to speak, are the very areas where you will most likely have the greatest impact. When you are working with your strengths, it is easy for you. You will usually be very efficient at completing the task. And the quality of your work will be high to boot. In other words everything will naturally work together for your success. On the other hand when you work in an area in which you are not gifted, it will be difficult, you won't be as efficient and the quality of your work will most likely not be up to par.

Think of someone with the gift of singing. They were born with melodious vocal cords. They have an ear for pitch and a range that easily takes in both the high and low notes. Singing is no chore at all. It's a joy for them to sing and likewise a joy for us to hear. On the other hand, many of us who would love to be able to sing can't carry a tune to save our lives. No matter how hard we try, it's not our gift.

When I think of someone who has been given a beautiful voice, Charlotte Church, the young lady from Ireland is the first person that comes to mind. When I first heard her sing, she was a young teenager. It was hard to believe that anyone so young could possibly produce such angelic tones. She clearly has a gift, which she has learned to use well.

What are your God given gifts and talents? Finding them

will add focus to your life.

Discovering your strengths

There are several elements that go into truly understanding your strengths and abilities. In the best selling book *The Purpose Driven Life* Rick Warren uses the word SHAPE as an acronym to outline those elements:

S– Spiritual gifts
H– Heart/Passions
A– Abilities
P– Personality
E– Experience

Dave Jewitt, who is the personal coach I mentioned in the preceding chapter, uses the acronym DESIGN.

D– Desires
E– Experience
S– Skills
I– Interests
G– Gifts (Spiritual)
N– Nature (Personality)

Both of these models use similar categories. Let's look at the DESIGN model to see how you can better define the unique "you."

Desires

When you wake up in the morning, what would you really like to do? What gives you a great sense of joy while you are doing it? You just love it! Desire is not the only word to describe this personal trait. What *drives* you? What are you *passionate* about? What do you have a *heart* for?

Make a list of everything you can remember that you have done that fits that pattern. Don't limit yourself only to those areas that earn money or any other limitation. Think as if you had no constraints. Money, time, health, etc. are not limiting. As you write down these various activities, patterns will begin to emerge. Once you have written down a whole page of joy-inducing activities, try to prioritize them and narrow the choices down to four or five that are the most exciting and motivating.

By the way, it's not always easy to know what your true desires are. Be patient with yourself. Take time to visit and then revisit this issue.

Experiences

Which of your life experiences have given you skills or knowledge that you can now apply to perform specific tasks or help others? While your desires always have a positive impact on you, experiences can be either positive or negative. Interestingly enough it is often the negative or painful experiences that teach us the most.

Many people's experiences don't line up perfectly with their heart and passions. So, although experiences can equip you in valuable ways, you should not limit your thinking to only those areas in which you have experience. Your family or financial situation may not have let you do what you really wanted. So, keep an open mind when it comes to experience. Work to distinguish the helpful experiences from the ones that weren't so helpful.

Skills

What are your God-given talents and abilities? Just as each of us is given a certain physical appearance that we can't easily change, we have also been given talents and abilities.

Each person's brain is wired differently. Some people are artistic. They see forms, colors and proportions that others don't. Others are mathematical and can easily see relationships between numbers.

My mother was trained as a classical pianist and organist. In fact, she was a church organist until her eightieth birthday. To this day she still plays the piano for chapel in her senior living center. You might think that I would have been blessed with some of her musical talent. You'd be wrong.

I tried to learn the piano, but it was no fun and I had no talent. I turned to the trombone and although I played well enough to be in the first few chairs in the trombone section, my ability was "mechanical." I could play notes put in front of me and even add some "feeling" in the process. But I had absolutely no ability to play by ear. The few musical successes I had came from hard work and struggle. I finally–happily–gave it up.

What are your talents? What do you find easy to do, which many others find a challenge?

Interests

Just because you have the ability to do something doesn't mean it is something you are interested in doing. Most people have talents in more than one area, but their interests may not match up perfectly with each of those abilities.

Where does your mind drift when you have nothing particular to think about? When you pick up the newspaper, what's the first section you turn to? If you were to take a class "just for fun," what area would it be in? These are where your natural interests lie.

Whatever your interest, you will find it easier to apply your talents and abilities to that area than others. No one has to push you or try to motivate you, because you're already self-motivated.

Gifts (Spiritual)

God has given you certain gifts so that you can have a spiritual impact on others. Many believe these gifts are given at the moment when you accept Jesus Christ as your Lord and Savior. While that may be true for some, it is also true that spiritual gifts often line up nicely with the natural talents and abilities God has given you.

You should use your spiritual gifts to minister to others. Those most often mentioned are the following:

- Healing–The gift to restore health to the sick.
- Intercession–The gift to pray for the building of the Kingdom.
- Hospitality–The gift to open your home and entertain others.
- Faith–The gift of great confidence in God's promises, power and presence.
- Discernment–The gift to know whether certain behavior is of God or Satan.
- Mercy–The gift of empathy and compassion for those who are suffering and to devote time and energy to alleviate it.
- Giving–The gift of offering material blessings for the work of God with great willingness, cheerfulness and liberality.
- Administration–The gift to organize and manage various aspects of the church's ministry.

- Leadership – The gift to direct and inspire God's people.
- Helps – The gift to bear other's burdens.
- Serving – The gift to serve others and help meet their needs.
- Knowledge – The gift of making God's truth relevant to everyday living in the Church.
- Exhortation – The gift to bring comfort, counsel and encouragement to others.
- Teacher – The gift of being able to teach others the truths of God's word.

When you look at what ministry or mission God might want you to do as a part of finishing well, it is important to know your spiritual gifts. There are short tests available to give insight into your spiritual gifts. (Check Google for "spiritual gifts tests.")

Nature / Personality

Each person has their own personality. Some are introverted. Some are extroverted. Some are natural-born comedians.

Imagine Henry Kissinger or Alan Greenspan taking Bob Hope's or David Letterman's place on a television show. It would be a disaster. No one would laugh – except at the absurdity of it all.

The importance of personality can also be seen in ministry settings. Suppose a talented young lady asked her church's missions committee to support her work in evangelism in a parachurch organization. Her heart was sincere, her motives pure, but everyone that knew her on the committee knew that she was painfully shy and retiring. They couldn't imagine her being outgoing enough to approach strangers and successfully build relationships. In this case the missions committee would be well advised to counsel her and question the wisdom of her decision.

Your God-given personality makes some situations easier and others harder for you to handle. Know your own personality in order to put yourself into the environment in which you will blossom. And remember, knowing yourself is a process that takes time. The longer you live, the more you develop your strengths, the more experiences you have, the better you will know yourself, your personality.

Put it all together

Once you've done a complete DESIGN analysis, put the pieces together. In what direction do they point?

If you have an outgoing personality and are good at speaking, you might do well as a teacher or in one of the performance areas, like radio or television. You might also do well in a position that requires a lot of presentations. Or, if you are more introverted, but gifted with a creative flair, you would probably do well in a profession that requires such right-brain talent.

The idea is to know who you are. What God has inherently designed you to do. What design God has given you?

You want the time you have left to count, no matter how short or long that time span may be. Once you truly know who you are, live your life like a rifle shot rather than a shotgun. Turn away from areas in which you will be only partially effective. Grab on to those areas and opportunities where your impact will be multiplied.

CHAPTER 10

Work – How We Got
Where We Are

The Elephant In The Living Room

Imagine gathering your family in the living room for a conversation one evening. As everyone comes in, you can't help but notice that right in the middle of the room is a full sized African elephant.

Can you even contemplate a conversation going on without anyone ever mentioning the elephant or asking what it was doing there? Of course not. And yet some discussions about life issues ignore the obvious. How could anyone talk about Social Security's future and not mention an aging population? How could any family talk about a young lady who was several months pregnant and not mention the coming baby?

It seems unbelievable, but we sometimes choose, for one reason or another, to ignore the obvious—the elephant in the living room.

When considering God's calling in and upon our lives, you have to take one particular elephant into account. One reality is so big that it shouldn't be ignored as you frame the balance of your life, yet it often is.

What is this elephant? Your work. Your job.

Work is such a big variable that we are going to spend the next three chapters on the topic. No unspoken elephant in this living room!

The vast majority of individuals cannot even consider stopping work, at least until they retire. And many find that they really cannot afford to retire completely either.

Does that mean that all these individuals cannot finish well? Does it mean that they have to wait until retirement to finish well?

Absolutely not. In fact work is a significant part of finishing well. Most spend more time at work than any other activity. They spend more time with co-workers than with family members.

Work is found everywhere, in all cultures and at all times in history. Depending on individual personalities and work experiences, each person struggles with this issue to a greater or lesser extent. Some love their work. It is both a joy to perform and results in a special sense of achievement and self-fulfillment. These individuals can easily become so focused on work that they neglect other areas in their lives. Others can become workaholics, using work to avoid life's other challenges or at least lead an unbalanced life.

At the other extreme, many people see work as a drudgery to be endured only because there is no other alternative. For them Friday can't arrive soon enough, and life tends to focus around leisure activities.

Work is more than a joy or burden. Indeed, from God's perspective, it is an integral part of life. It is important to understand why God made work such a large part of our existence. What is the value of work? What is God trying to accomplish in and through it? And, for many, the question of "what work does God want me to do?" can consume many waking hours.[2]

You can't set out to finish well if you don't know how work fits into your plan.

---

2 In developing and preparing these thoughts on work I read several books and many articles. The most comprehensive presentation of the issues on work was in the book, *Work & Leisure in Christian Perspective* by Leland Ryken. If you are interested in pursuing this topic more thoroughly, I would recommend you get a copy of Mr. Ryken's book. Of course, as followers of Jesus Christ we should always use the Bible as our final authority. Although many sources can enhance and add to our thinking, ultimately nothing we settle on should be in conflict with the values, principles, or tenets put forth in the Bible. It is our final authority on faith and conduct. Many passages of Scripture directly address the subject of work. In addition, much can be learned indirectly by looking at the lives of those in Scripture.

Work Defined

Although man's view of work has changed over the centuries, God's view hasn't. The next few pages will provide some perspective–and some lessons from history–to help you determine the role work should play in the remaining years of your life.

The first step to understanding work and God's purpose in work is to define it. Many varied activities make up our waking hours. Some of those we would call our job activities–those things we do that we get paid for. Others are done purely because we choose to do them. That contrast is the basis for understanding what work is versus what is considered leisure.

Work is something we are obligated to do–and most often are paid to do it. If we don't perform the required tasks there are consequences.

Leisure, on the other hand, is something we choose to do because it gives us pleasure. If we don't, there is no significant consequence. Leisure can be a recreational activity, an educational experience, or entertainment. The common thread is the freedom to choose to do it or not.

Many activities don't strictly fit either the work or leisure categories. They fall in between. You are not going to get fired if you don't do them, but you still have some obligation to get them done. Household chores usually are in this area–probably more obligation than choice. Other activities might be more choice than obligation, but nonetheless impose some demands on your daily life. For example, you might choose to own a swimming pool for the pleasure it brings.

But, cleaning the pool then becomes an obligation, which you might not enjoy doing every time.

There are many reasons we perform work:

- To earn money to provide a standard of living

- To accomplish a task

- To achieve a goal

- To find a sense of self-fulfillment

- To be of service to others

Work—The Problem

The number one reason most people work is to make a living. We dream of financial freedom, but for most individuals that is all it will ever be—a dream. They never break free from the gravitational pull of financial need and out into the orbit of financial freedom. Even retirement may not bring the financial freedom desired unless an individual is able to save a considerable amount before retirement.

Piled on top of the need to earn a living is the issue of your standard of living. Most of us find it hard to resist the constant push to live above our means. We go into debt to acquire and then find ourselves having to work longer hours or multiple jobs to pay the bills. Work can easily become a burden.

In a very real sense, those who learn to live under their income are the wealthiest regardless of the level of their income.

No matter how the issue may be sugar coated, work is

still…work. It requires varying amounts of physical effort and often is drudgery.

Most religious people of the Judeo-Christian heritage think of work in the context of the curse given when man fell into sin. Genesis 3:17-19 says, "Cursed is the ground because of you; through painful toil you will eat of it all the days of your life…By the sweat of your brow you will eat your food…" This passage alone puts a negative focus on work.

Many make the mistake of thinking that this is where work entered the picture and it was drudgery from the start. However, that is not true. God actually established work before man sinned. Genesis 2:15 says, "The Lord God took the man and put him in the Garden of Eden to work it and take care of it." Work was present from the beginning, but we will never know what that work was like before sin entered the world.

Although the overall view of work usually leans toward the negative side, it doesn't have to. Work certainly is productive and good—we talk about wanting a good "work ethic" in our children and in society in general—however, most long for less work and more leisure.

Bumper sticker philosophy is a good barometer of our underlying feelings concerning work.

- I'd rather be…skiing, golfing, hunting, etc.

- Work fascinates me. I can watch it for hours.

- Work won't kill you, but I'm not taking any chances.

Whoever saw a bumper sticker that said, "Thank God It's Monday!"

Work – a Mixed Bag

The challenge presented by work is that it brings a variety of outcomes. It certainly can be a curse or drudgery. However, it can also bring great joy through the production of wonderful products, the giving of a sense of accomplishment and self worth, and by being a means through which to serve others.

And while work can create certain problems, the lack of work can be even worse. Unemployment or underemployment can be devastating. We all know someone who has lost a job and looked unsuccessfully to find an appropriate replacement. They suffer tremendously, going through a sense of boredom and worthlessness that can lead to depression and in some cases suicide.

At the other end of the scale is leisure. Most feel it brings quality to life. However, excess leisure has its own set of problems such as boredom, loneliness, and depression as well. We are all aware of the many devastated lives in the entertainment industry, which often creates a lifestyle with extended periods of leisure time between work activities. Excess leisure often leads to drug or alcohol abuse or sexual dalliances. Soon relationships are on the line. Marriages fail and families are pulled apart. Have you ever heard the old saying, "Idle hands are the devil's playground"? That's precisely the danger behind too much leisure.

The solution to the challenge of work is uniquely found by looking at God's intention for work. However, before we address that we will take a brief look at the past.

Historical attitudes toward work

We learn by knowing history. How we got to where we are. It is not only enlightening; it can also help us avoid some of the mistakes of the past.

Our culture finds its historical roots in the Greek and Roman eras, as well as Judeo-Christian beliefs and values. Each of them contributes significantly toward our view of work today.

The Greeks saw work as a curse. Working was thought to be beneath the dignity of a "free man." It was supposed to be carried out by slaves, craftsmen and laborers. What made a person noble was the freedom to exercise the mind in the areas of art, philosophy, and politics. The Roman view was very similar. Work was for the lower classes.

It is important to note that the Greek and Roman view of work grew out of a social structure that approved of and promoted slavery. In addition, the philosophy of the day held a low view of the physical world. Activities of the mind were valued above all else.

Judaic and Christian heritage defined work a bit more generously. Because slavery was not the foundation of the social structure, work had to be viewed as appropriate for everybody. Even so, work did not exactly rate a place of honor in society. Essentially, work was divided into sacred and secular.

Sacred work was exalted. Secular work, though necessary, was held in much lower esteem. Unfortunately this legacy from the Middle Ages, remains alive and well today in both Catholic and Protestant circles.

The Renaissance and the Reformation raised work to a

higher plain. The humanism of the Renaissance believed in the dignity of human work and placed special value on what it could achieve. Praising work lifted it out of its historical mire.

Even more important than the Renaissance was the Reformation. Luther, Calvin, and the Puritans brought about the "Protestant work ethic." The division of work into sacred and secular was rejected. The belief that God "called" people to perform work made all work done for God and His glory sacred. Industriousness and profit became acceptable, and even desired. Although the Protestant work ethic has been distorted in the centuries since, it actually gave common work a higher place and greater dignity than it ever had before or since.

The Enlightenment secularized the Protestant work ethic. Separating the work ethic from its Christian context turned the focus away from God and toward personal success. Work was rooted not in service to God, but in personal achievement to get ahead. (This secular work ethic is what most people–incorrectly–think of as the Protestant work ethic.) Adam Smith and John Locke were proponents of this new work ethic.

The Industrial Revolution of the nineteenth century took this work ethic to a new place. Industrialization brought specialization to work and, sadly, abuse of the worker. The inevitable result was the alienation of the worker. Marx saw the problem, but came up with the wrong solution. Some secular movements such as Victorianism and Romanticism also saw the problem and tried to lift work back up to a noble position. But, in general, they had to–or just did–ignore the factory worker.

Today there is no common view of work. It is seen as fulfilling a variety of needs or purposes from utilitarian – getting a job done – to a part of self actualization. For the most part it is viewed as secular. However, exactly how it is viewed depends upon the position of the particular worker. To the craftsman work is noble and fruitful. To the professional it can be fulfilling, and even become the major driving point of their lives. To the 8 to 5 worker, common laborer, or even the homemaker work is often a drudgery that has to be put up with in order to provide other necessities of life, as well as the means to enjoy the pleasures that life can offer.

History shows the pitfalls and dead ends of the different views of work. Not surprisingly the popular view of work often found at a particular time in history usually formed its foundation from the views of the power structure of that particular society. In the Greek and Roman eras work was viewed as bad because slaves performed it. In the Middle Ages, when the clergy dominated society, sacred work was viewed as more noble than secular work. Today, with the free market winning the world, most people see work in economic terms. Humanism wants individuals to be fulfilled and self-actualized, however, in those circumstances where fulfillment is questionable, proper compensation and good working conditions are the goals.

While the dominant perspectives on work changes right along with the prevalent worldview of different societies, we need to remember that God is the same yesterday, today and forever. God's view of work does not change. It is critical that we understand what His view is.

If we are going to find the meaning for work that we desire, it is clear that work needs to have its roots in the God who created it and intended it for His purposes. The main source of authority for that view must be the Bible. We need to base our view on an eternal foundation, not on the beliefs and practices of a particular passing culture.

God is a working God

Throughout Scripture God is seen carrying out His work. Genesis 1:1 opens the Bible with "In the beginning God created the heavens and the earth." God is at work. The Bible finishes in Revelation with God completing His work of redemption. Throughout Scripture God is working to sustain his creation, bring His providence into play, judge the actions of man, and bring redemption.

Jesus talked about God's work. In John 4:34 he said, "My food is to do the will of him who sent me and to finish his work." In John 5:17 Jesus said, "My Father is always at his work to this very day, and I, too, am working." And, in John 9:4 he said, " ... we must do the work of him who sent me."

God is a working God. That fact alone gives dignity to work.

Implications of a working God

First, we were created in God's image. Genesis 1:27 "God created man in his own image ... " As a part of that image man was created to work. The fact that both God and man are workers is referred to in the Ten Commandments. Exodus 20:8-11 refers to the fact that man is to work six days and rest the seventh, just like God did at the time of creation.

Second, work is a mandate from God. Genesis 1:26 "...let them (man) rule over the fish of the sea and the birds of the air, over the livestock, over all the earth, and over all the creatures that move along the ground." Dominion over the earth means "work." Work is assumed throughout the Bible. In Psalm 104:19-23 work is compared to the rising and setting of the sun. It is daily. It is common. It is expected. The main reason we work is because that is God's plan for man.

Third, work was to be pleasant and necessary. In Genesis 2:15 God put man in the Garden of Eden to work it and take care of it. This was before man sinned (the fall of man). Work was part and parcel of the world God had created for man in its pristine state.

Finally, God and man work together. Psalm 127:1 says that unless God is involved, the work is done in vain. God establishes our work (Psalm 90:17). His partnership in the work brings value and meaning to work. Martin Luther said that it is important to understand this partnership in work between man and God because it saves us from the fear of ineffectiveness, as well as from arrogance over human achievement.

Work as a curse
Because work is often toil and burdensome, it is easy to think of it as not the best way to spend time. That is exactly what the Greeks and Romans thought. Work was for slaves and the lower classes. However, we know from God's example and his mandate that work was not designed to be a lower task. Where did our perspective get so far off track?

In part, man's sin changed the picture. Genesis 3:17-19 says, "Cursed is the ground because of you; through painful toil you will eat of it all the days of your life. It will produce thorns and thistles for you, and you will eat the plants of the field. By the sweat of your brow you will eat your food…"

The fall did not introduce work, but it did introduce toil. It fundamentally changed work, but it did not do away with the necessity and duty to perform it.

The redemption of work

A part of God's plan to redeem man from his sinful condition extends to the physical world and work. Work does not have to be cursed. It's doesn't always have to be toil. It can be redeemed and bring joy and meaning back into the life of the worker. Beyond giving us a basis for work, the Bible gives hope. It sheds light on how we are to live and work in a fallen world.

CHAPTER 11

Work – No More Sacred Versus Secular

Common work is glorified

After reading Scripture you are compelled to agree with the Reformers who regarded everything as sacred. The view that a life of devotion is superior is flatly rejected. Everyday life was the playing field on which God encountered man. Our entire life, both secular and sacred, is spiritual. We need to reject any notion of a separation between our "church life" and our "work life the rest of the week." We take our faith with us into church and equally into the workplace or wherever else we are. How we express that faith changes with the environment, but not the fact that faith is there, which forms the basis of our lives.

Paul says that we do everything to the glory of God. Therein lies a wonderful blessing. Work that normally would be drudgery, when viewed as being done for God's glory, brings fulfillment and even enjoyment.

The practical outcome

Although society may reward different types of work differently, God views everyone's work equally when it is done for his glory. That's right, God says that every type of work is important–whether it is teaching a college class in higher mathematics or picking up the trash.

How many times have you thanked God for the food at your table? He promises to provide. Let's take a moment and think about how that provision is made. By what means does God get food on your table?

- God uses the farmer to grow it
- The factory worker who makes the farm equipment for the farmer
- The tool and die worker who makes the equipment to run the factory that in turn makes the farm equipment
- The doctors and nurses who provide health care for the farmers and factory workers
- The oil companies and electric utilities who provide the

farmer with power

- The truck drivers who pick up the raw food and bring it to the processor
- The processor who packages the food
- The grocery store workers who distribute it to the local store
- The local cashier who checks you out when you buy the food
- The appliance manufacturer who makes your stove
- And the list can go on and on...

Knowing that God is using them to make provision brings dignity to every part of the work chain.

We could trace a similar process for shelter, clothing and even intangibles such as justice and concern for the poor.

The Bible clearly teaches God's desire for justice in the world. We are told in Isaiah 30 verse 18 that God loves justice. Therefore, it is clear that lawyers (yes, even lawyers!), judges, policemen, and prison workers are a significant part of the fabric by which God brings justice to the world.

A local church wouldn't function well without someone to clean and maintain it. The mercy of God is seen through the healing skills of physicians and nurses. And, they couldn't do their work without the hospital support staff... or the laundries that do the linens... or ambulance drivers that bring in critical patients... or the pharmaceutical companies that manufacture the drugs.

If you are doing your work just for a paycheck, you are missing out. You should be working for God. God is your audience, not just your boss, coworkers, or customers.

What about calling?

It's the next question that naturally arises. Doesn't the Bible specifically speak about a calling to certain professions? It does, but that's only a part of the story. Paul, for example, was called by God to be an apostle. Others, like Abraham, were called to perform specific tasks, not all related to the sacred. However, there is a higher call than the call to work.

By far the most important "calling" of Scripture is to salvation, and the ensuing life that is committed to God. This is a general calling of God and supersedes all other callings. In the Old Testament Abraham was called into a covenant with God that included the whole nation of Israel. They were all called to follow God. In the New Testament the call is to individuals to follow God.

Paul talks about this many times in his epistles. In I Corinthians 1:9 he talks about being "called into the fellowship of [God's] Son, Jesus Christ our Lord." In other passages he talks about being called "to be saved." (I Thessalonians 2:13, 14.) This primary calling of God demonstrates that all of life should be surrounded and motivated by the spiritual. Work is included under this general calling to a life committed to God.

Second to the general call to Salvation, the Bible also talks about being called to religious service. The prophets were called by God to perform a specific task. In the New Testament Paul talks about being called to various religious positions that required the use of spiritual gifts that had been given–prophets, teachers, administrators, healers, etc. (Ephesians 4:11 and I

Corinthians 12:28.) It is clear that God calls some individuals to perform work related to religious activities.

The Reformation expanded the use of "calling" to apply to occupations outside the religious. They looked at various passages that revealed God actively calling (seeking, asking, choosing, commanding) individuals to do things that were not religious in nature. He called Saul and David to lead a nation. He called Bezalel to be a craftsman filled with the Spirit of God. (Exodus 31:1-6.) In I Corinthians 7 Paul says that an individual should lead "the life which the Lord assigned to him and in which God has called him ... " Jesus affirmed the basic value of professions in Luke 3:12-14 when he told tax collectors being baptized to go back to collecting taxes, but not to take more that they are supposed to. Clearly, faith brings a new dimension to the workplace but it does not deny the necessity and appropriateness of the work.

Faith is the foundation of all work

The general call of God to salvation is the most important calling for each person. Faith becomes the foundation upon which the rest of life is built. To understand the appropriate view of work for the believer, you must put work into the framework of God's primary call to salvation and a life devoted to Him. Work then takes on a new significance.

First, because God is the one who is calling the person to work. Second, because the work is being done in response to God's call.

God's call to work in the life of the believer changes the whole fabric of work. It may still be hard, but it no longer has to be drudgery. God calls us to work and serve Him in the process. Consequently, all work to which the believer is called has a spiritual dimension. The significance of any given task does not spring from the task itself, but rather from the person for whom the work is done.

Spiritual significance is the great equalizer that puts all workers on the same level in the eyes of God. Add to this the knowledge that all fellow believers are your brothers and sisters in Christ, regardless of profession, and you have the basis to view everyone as your equal before God. All legitimate work has significance and contributes to the well being of mankind.

No sacred/secular division

The earth is the Lords. He owns the cattle on a thousand hills and the wealth in every mine. The Protestant work ethic viewed every area of work as equal from a spiritual standpoint. All work (except that which is a contradiction to holy living), from the lowliest job to the loftiest, is pleasing to God. Paul said in I Corinthians 10:31, "So, whether you eat or drink, or whatever you do, do all to the glory of God."

Common work is raised to a level of dignity because we are doing it for God's glory. There is no distinction between sacred and secular. The Apostle Paul is a prime example. He clearly declares that he has been called by God to be an Apostle and also explains that it is only right for a minister to be supported financially. However, at times Paul chose to support himself by the making of tents. Of all people he could have opted for totally spiritual work, and yet he chose to continue working in a secular role as well.

As you read Scripture you encounter people involved many types of secular work. It is never derided as "less spiritual." David was a shepherd and later the King. Today's version would be the head of a country, or a politician. There were garment makers, chariot drivers, farmers, judges, business people, tax collectors, physicians and many others. Job, the wealthiest man of his time, was looked upon by God with extreme favor, and he was a landowner, who raised livestock. The more you read Scripture the more examples you have of common people, doing common work, who were praised for their faithfulness in the midst of their vocation.

Some of the great heroes of Scripture worked in the secular realm. Joseph is a prime example. He never worked at a sacred profession. Yet he always worked for the glory of God, whether as a slave, a prisoner or leading the country to prepare for famine. Then there was Abraham, who is revered for his obedience to God. He led a nation as a nomad with flocks.

Jesus was a common worker

The ultimate example comes from Jesus himself. He was a carpenter from youth to about 30 years of age. He supported himself and family through the work of his hands. He made no distinction between those who worked at sacred professions or secular. In fact, his criticism was more often aimed against the sacred professional rather than the secular worker.

CHAPTER 12

Work – Your Role

How can you know what God wants you to do?
Nowhere does Scripture give any specific counsel concerning how to select a vocation. So, guidance in this area has to come from implication and application of general Scriptural principles.

In I Timothy 3 Paul talks about God given gifts that make a person suitable for a specific spiritual task. By implication we can assume that God also gives talents, aptitudes, and personalities that are particularly suited to certain professions.

Calling or feeling

God gave us our minds and the ability to reason. We should use this intellect in the process of selecting our work. There is a tendency in many religious circles to want to be able to say, "I feel God led me" to make a certain decision. In fact, there seems to be a universal human "desire" to be led by a mysterious, outside force. We need to be careful that we don't abdicate personal decision-making responsibility, at the altar of "feeling." Certainly, God can, and does, lead us through the Holy Spirit. Some are so moved and drawn with a sense of calling to a certain task or profession, that they can explain it by nothing else than God leading them. However, not everyone has that experience, and even those that do should question their feelings.

Does the work you feel you are being called to do align with the principles of a Godly life as outlined in the Bible? Doug Cole is a good friend and strong believer, who owned and operated a restaurant in Springfield, Oregon. He helped me through some very difficult challenges many years ago and I value his insight and counsel. He once told me, "When I feel called to do something, I need to remember that it might be God ... or it might be pizza."

Doug has trained himself to question his feelings by confirming that the resulting action or task would be in conformity with Biblical principles. For example, one day you might feel like socking your neighbor in the nose. On another day you might feel a need to apologize and reconcile. Carrying through on the first feeling would be against Biblical principles, while the second would align with them.

Circumstance

Another significant factor in selecting a profession is circumstances. How a person gets one job versus another is normally the result of a combination of many varied circumstances that God places or allows in their lives. Just like Robert Frost's road that diverged in a yellow wood, one decision leads on to another, and when put together they make all the difference. Look at your talents, aptitudes, personality, and circumstances and then pray that God would lead the process of selecting your field of work and a specific job. He will, and you can have confidence in the conclusion that God has been involved throughout.

One practical piece of advice: once you have prayerfully and thoughtfully made a decision with the best ability you have, don't second guess yourself. Always live in the present–where you are today–and move forward depending upon God's continued leading.

Stewardship in work

Another practical aspect of God's redemption of work is that we are called to be stewards of what has been entrusted to us. It is true of possessions, skills or talents. We are called to be stewards of His possessions and His work, as well as the abilities He has given us.

When it comes to stewardship, Scripture has given us very clear guidance. The parable of the talents teaches our responsibilities well (Matthew 25:14-30). Three servants were given different amounts of money by their master. Two of them doubled the amounts by the time the master returned. The third hid it in the ground so as not to lose it. The first two were commended for their stewardship. They were praised and rewarded. The third was condemned for not being a good steward.

There are several points we can take from this parable.

First, God gave each one something to be a steward over.

God gives us talents, abilities, aptitudes, and opportunities over which we are to be stewards. It is a part of our service to Him.

Second, He doesn't give the same amounts to each person.

Whether it's time on earth, talents, opportunities or possessions, some get more of one than another might get. That doesn't change the need to be a good and faithful steward over whatever mix you've been given.

Third, the same results are not required of everyone.

The results were based upon what had been entrusted. God judges not based purely on results, but what you've done with the talents and abilities you have been given. Those who have been given much will be expected to produce more than those that have been given less.

Fourth, *there are rewards for good stewardship.*

Those rewards may or may not be monetary. In the case of these servants, they were given proportionately more over which to be stewards, i.e. even more responsibility. The reward was that they were praised by the master and allowed to serve even more.

Finally, *each person has a choice about whether or not to be a good steward.*

God never takes away your ability to choose. You can choose daily how you will or will not serve Him.

The principle of stewardship is the final piece to the puzzle of the redemption of work. Two Scriptures summarize how stewardship changes the focus and makes the task, no matter how humble, a service to God.

Colossians 3:23-24. "Whatever you do, work at it with all your heart, as working for the Lord, not for men, since you know that you will receive an inheritance from the Lord as a reward. It is the Lord Christ you are serving."

Ephesians 6:7. "Serve wholeheartedly, as if you were serving the Lord, not men, because you know that the Lord will reward everyone for whatever good he does."

God's purpose for work

Work is important from man's perspective. It has utilitarian value in providing the necessities and pleasures for living. It is a means of fulfillment and satisfaction. Through work we serve mankind. And, most important we serve God in and through our work. God certainly had all these in mind when he made work an integral part of the human experience. However, he also uses work as a significant element in his plan of redemption.

Matthew 5:13, 14: "You are the salt of the earth... You are the light of the world." Believers are placed everywhere throughout society as salt and light to the world. God doesn't just want his followers confined to churches. That's like keeping salt in the shaker or keeping a light hidden under a bushel. To be useful, the salt has to be spread about. Like salt, the believer is a preservative in society.

By becoming more like Christ through the power of the Holy Spirit, the believer preserves the moral climate. And, through following the commandment to love his neighbor, the believer adds a beautiful flavor wherever he goes. God's people roll back the darkness by standing as a beacon for truth and justice.

God needs his followers everywhere. In fact, the vast majority of His ministers work in the secular world. It takes believers like you and me to reach many, if not most,

146

non-believers.

Look at the various buildings in your city as you drive by. God needs His people at city hall, every school, each hospital, library, fire station, restaurant, and business establishment. Wherever there are people, God wants his people there too. Even in horrible places like concentration camps God's people can make a great difference. (Read about what God did in the concentration camps in Corey TenBoom's autobiography *The Hiding Place*.)

When you think of the workplace, remember God created all, and is sovereign over all.

In our modern day the church has been marginalized to the periphery of society. It no longer stands at the center as it used to. More than ever before the workplace is a key platform to reach modern man with the Gospel of Jesus Christ. God extends his grace to the world through the living witness of his followers.

In seminary theology students are taught not just about the saving grace of God through which man can be forgiven of sins and redeemed, but also about the common (general) grace of God through which God restrains evil in the world.

Chuck Colson says that the greatest myth pushed on modern man is the "goodness of man." The idea of original sin has been swept aside in a tide of self-focused, prideful thinking. Nonetheless, man proves his true orientation daily. Colson says that the line between good and evil is not found with a Hitler on one side and a Mother Teresa on the other.

The line between good and evil goes right through the heart of every man and woman. Without the restraint offered by the grace of God over all of society, we would all land continually on the evil side of that line.

No theological concept is more born out by history than that of the sinfulness of man. No century in the history of man has had more torture and killing of man by his fellowman than the twentieth century. If you want to see the true nature of man, look at a child who is undisciplined. Self-centeredness and selfishness dominate. But because of his love for mankind, God covers the world with his common grace to restrain evil. The believer in the workplace is an integral part of God's common grace.

Keep God at the center

As you go about your daily work, remember it is God ordained. Do your work unto the Lord. Enjoy it. Use it to provide for your needs. Succeed at it. Accomplish as much as you can. However, do it all with your eyes fixed upon Jesus Christ, your savior and Lord. The common purpose of all believers, as found in Matthew 22:37–39, applies directly to your work and work environment.

"Jesus replied: "'Love the Lord your God with all your heart and with all your soul and with all your mind.' This is the first and greatest commandment. And the second is like it: 'Love your neighbor as yourself.'"

The reward for work well done

In I Corinthians 3:11 the Apostle Paul says, "For no one can lay any foundation other than the one already laid, which is Jesus Christ. If any man builds on this foundation using gold, silver, costly stones, wood, hay or straw, his work will be shown for what it is, because the Day will bring it to light. It will be revealed with fire, and the fire will test the quality of each man's work. If what he has built survives, he will receive his reward."

If you do your work for Jesus Christ, not only will you be blessed in this life with satisfaction, contentment and a great sense of fulfillment, but also you will receive a reward in the next.

Working to finish well

Because work is such a major part of almost everyone's life, finishing well has to incorporate work as a major part of the finishing well plan. In order to do that, you need to see work as more than providing a paycheck or an opportunity to get ahead. It needs to be seen as one of your major venues in which you become salt and light for God. He's becomes your central motivation and your primary audience.

Your time frame changes from now-until-retirement to eternity. Mentally remove the line in your life that marks the change from life on earth to life in heaven. What you are doing can and should have an eternal impact in your life as well as the lives of others. See your work as a calling from God himself to bring moral character and fiber into your workplace, as well as a witness to what He can do in the lives of those who will trust Him.

What about retirement?

As workers get older in modern western culture they almost universally look forward to retirement. It's seen as a time when they can relax, get away from the grind of a work schedule, and devote their time to leisure activities. It sounds attractive. However, how it plays out is usually a different story.

It is common that men who retire to do nothing but leisure usually end up bored and, what's more, they often don't live as long. Retirement can be bad for your health–mental and physical. Remember, God created you in His image and a significant part of that image is work. Most people just don't function as well without it.

Nowhere in the Bible is retirement mentioned. In fact, the idea of retirement is fairly new on the historical scene. Most people throughout history have worked right on up to disability, declining health or death. It's only the affluent western society, which has made the idea of retirement financially possible for the middle class.

If you want a vibrant retirement and longer life, stay active. Staying active does not mean that you need to keep a 9 to 5 job and keep earning a living. For some that will be a necessity, but for many others it won't. If your financial situation allows, it's ok to stop working for pay. However, to be healthy and productive you need to find other activities to do that go beyond pure leisure.

If you want to finish well in retirement, you need to view retirement as another opportunity to be a steward of the talents and abilities that God has given you to penetrate the world you live in for Jesus Christ. You might volunteer or you might combine volunteering and working part-time. It may be in the sacred or secular world. But whatever you do, it will get its primary purpose from serving Jesus Christ.

CHAPTER 13

Success and Finishing Well

Good created men with a drive to succeed and win. It's a part of our testosterone programming. As a result it is perfectly natural for men to set out to provide for their families and become successful. Long hours and hard work are often a part of the program.

However, as midlife approaches, it is normal to discover that there is emptiness inside that success hasn't fulfilled. It's that God-shaped hole. That void deep in everyone that can only be filled by the Lord's presence. By midlife most of us have tried just about everything to fill the hole and nothing has lasted. Money, power, fame all work temporarily, but soon wear off. With the end of life now appearing on the horizon, you may, perhaps for the first time, yearn to do something that has lasting value. Something greater than prosperity, power or prestige.

Instead of building buildings for profit, you might turn to building churches or take a short-term missionary project to build a church in another part of the world. You might focus on relationships or teaching or even a change of professions to move into a work that has a more direct impact on the lives of others. Work or activities that do more to help others than merely sell them a product or service.

Choosing to do something that has lasting value is very understandable and desirable. It's a good idea and holds the potential of making life much more fulfilling. It can be an integral part of structuring your life to finish well. However, be aware that simply turning your energies to tasks with some lasting value will not ultimately fulfill your desire to finish well. That may be a good technique, but it's not the strategy.

Finishing well primarily involves focusing on doing what God wants you to do. Wherever you are and whatever you do, you do it for His glory and His purposes. The driving force is the realization that whatever it is, it's what God wants you to do.

If it's what God wants you to do, you will find yourself happy and satisfied. I remember as a young person thinking that I would do anything God wanted me to do, but I sure didn't want it to be on a mission field in Africa. I have since come to realize that if God called me to do that, he would plant the desire in my heart and I would only find true happiness and satisfaction serving as a missionary. I really didn't have to worry about what or where God wanted me, because along with the mission would come the desire and fulfillment I was seeking.

And no surprise, for several years now I have been involved with a mission in Tanzania, Africa, which has brought tremendous joy, as well as growth to my spiritual life.

Finding the right work

Look as hard as you can. No where will you find a list of "approved" activities that God wants men to do in order to finish well. The importance or eternal value of a given job or task comes not from what the task is about so much as the value God places on it. The value is "in the eye of the beholder" – and in this case the beholder is God Himself.

You don't have to leave your current profession to finish well. Although that may be true for some, it is not true for most. Nor do you have to leave your current position in order to find the correct playing field on which to finish well. You may only have to look at what you are doing differently with a different set of eyes. How is God at work in what you are doing? What can you do for God where you are?

For example: one individual may start and operate a business that brings jobs and income to support a hundred families. Another person starts a homeless shelter that also helps a hundred families. The tendency would be to view the

homeless shelter as offering more eternal value and possibly
a better place to work to finish well. After all, God tells us to
take care of the poor.

However, every job that is in keeping with the moral
principles given in the Bible can be performed for the glory
of God. In this example the first person is contributing to the
quality of lives of one hundred employees, their families and
customers as well. This is very good work. God needs his men
everywhere to be salt and light and spread the Gospel through
example, deeds and words.

So, don't think that finishing well means you have to find
some other kind of work that exists somewhere "out there."
No matter where you find yourself, you are a part spreading
the Gospel of Jesus Christ and you are His hands and feet in
bringing His love to the people God has put around you. You are
a part of the salt and light He wants spread throughout society.

In fact, most men looking to finish well will stay put in their
current profession or work. They have credibility, experience,
as well as respect from and for peers and customers. They are
probably efficient at what they do and produce work with high
quality, because of their experience and from utilizing the gifts
and talents they have. Serving God where you are can bring
great joy and yield God-sized results when God is allowed to
be at the center.

Living well and finishing well

I don't believe God waits patiently until we are at midlife to
want us to do something special with our time and energy.
Rather, I believe all of life is to be lived for Him and He has a

plan for each one of us that will bring fulfillment, success and eternal value to whatever season of life you find yourself in.

My father was a Baptist minister. I can remember him saying on more than one occasion:

"If you want to be graceful and kind when you are eighty, you need to be graceful and kind when you are seventy. And, if you want to be graceful and kind when you are seventy, you need to be graceful and kind when you are sixty. And, if you want to be graceful and kind when you are sixty, you need to be graceful and kind when you are fifty. You don't all of a sudden wake up one morning, change a few things and become graceful and kind. It's a life-long practice that you do through the strength of God living within you."

Finishing well is just like gracefulness and kindness. You don't have to wait until you're forty or fifty to begin to think about finishing well. You need to finish each decade of your life well by living for God in the beings and doings of each phase of your life. For example, shouldn't you desire to finish well as a parent when you're in the parenting years? Of course! Parenting is one of the greatest tasks given to us by God. To raise and train children in the love of God is a primary calling for young couples.

At the same time, it is true that when a man hits midlife and sees more clearly that his time on earth is short, he has a renewed desire to make sure the time that is left is not wasted. Only what is done for God will count. Only the treasures you store up in heaven will be there when you get there.

God made you to desire success and be successful. God

also made you to desire to do things that have eternal value. Just as he made you to desire a physical relationship with your spouse and to enjoy the fulfillment of that physical relationship, He also gives you other desires to be fulfilled and enjoyed. He made us to desire many things that we are capable of fulfilling. He is pleased in our doing so. But none of them will bring ultimate satisfaction.

Some might define finishing well as being successful in your chosen career. A well-deserved obituary shows you finished well. Some might define finishing well as maintaining close relationships up to the end. Others might define finishing well as making a contribution back to the community you lived in.

As nice and important as each of those life elements is, they do not in and of themselves capture the essence of finishing well. The reality is both much simpler and much more profound.

PART IV

Putting It All Together

CHAPTER 14

The Conclusion

In the preceding thirteen chapters we looked at the idea of finishing well from various perspectives. The following are the key points that were covered:

- You were made to finish well. You have a God-shaped hole that can only be filled by God. Then he leads you to live according to the way He created you.
- The most common roads taken to bring satisfaction and

finish well don't work. Money, success, sex, power, fame and materialism will never meet the needs you have within you to finish well.

- Finishing well is not something you achieve once and for all. Like life itself, finishing well is a journey and must be addressed each and every day of your life.
- Live with a focus on eternity, not your short life here on earth. Only an eternal perspective can shift your focus to what is really important.
- Put your focus on God, not yourself. He created you for His purpose.
- Desire to become like Jesus Christ. Know Him. Love Him. Let Him live in and through you. Follow His teachings.
- Evaluate and settle on your principles of living and commit them to writing. These principles become your "non-negotiables." They also form the filter through which you see and interpret the world. They come from your worldview. A view in which God created everything, He has a plan and purpose for you, and He has set down immutable laws by which life is to be lived.
- See the world in a way that reflects your beliefs about God.
- Remember both the qualitative and quantitative aspect of the doings of life. Keep God and relationships at the forefront.
- To finish well you must understand how God created you. You are uniquely designed or shaped to fulfill a certain role. You need to know who you are.
- Work comprises more of your time than any other activity.

Finishing well must include your work if it is to be practical and involve your total life.

- Retirement is not a good option if it's focused on self and leisure.
- You should pursue finishing well in every season of your life.
- Perspective makes all the difference. Your motivation for doing what you do is a significant part of finishing well in your work. You don't have to change job or vocation to finish well. But you may have to change your perspective.

Living a quiet life

In I Thessalonians 4:11 Paul says, "Make it your ambition to lead a quiet life, to mind your own business and to work with your hands, just as we told you, so that your daily life may win the respect of outsiders and so that you will not be dependent on anybody."

You don't have to become the best or most famous businessman, teacher, preacher or _____ (you fill in the blank). Yes, excel. Be a good and faithful steward of the talents, abilities and personality God has given you. Do everything for Him with diligence and excellence. But your goal is not the excellence itself; it's stewardship and service.

Remember, life-changing events most often come along in the midst of ordinary, everyday activities and decisions. Sometimes you don't even know they were life changing until after the fact. If you walk daily with a focus on service to God–doing what He wants you to do–you don't have to worry about the big stuff. The daily journey will add up to a life of purpose centered on His will for your life.

Finishing well defined
"Well done good and faithful servant."

Jesus words in Matthew 25:21 lay out the challenge and the reward we all seek. Imagine God commending you for the life you have lived. Leading such a life that you can look forward to hearing those words when you enter God's presence. Make that your goal in life.

You will never be able to finish well on your own power and according to the typical goals of this world. Others might think you finished well, but they don't count. Only God counts.

Your goal needs to be to live for Him. It's all about God, letting Jesus Christ into your heart, becoming like Jesus Christ through His work in your life, and doing His will. Your goal? To have your Lord and savior say to you, "Well done my good and faithful servant." That's all that ultimately matters.

Many small individual steps make a direction...and a direction becomes a life path. No matter where you are today or what your life has been like so far, you *can* finish well–one day at a time. Starting today, turn your eyes heavenward and live your life for Him. Finish each day well...and in the end you certainly will hear the words...

Well done, good and faithful servant!

To contact the author:
Paul Goodman can be reached at
www.plgoodman@aol.com